RICHER'S
LEGAL
NUGGETS

RICHER'S LEGAL NUGGETS

A money-saving guide to everyday legal problems

Percy Richer
with illustrations by Simon Bond

A Queen Anne Press BOOK

© text: The Estate of Percy Richer 1987
© illustrations: Simon Bond 1987

First published in Great Britain in 1987 by
Queen Anne Press, a division of
Macdonald & Co (Publishers) Ltd
3rd Floor
Greater London House
Hampstead Road
London NW1 7QX

A BPCC plc Company

British Library Cataloguing in Publication Data

Richer, Percy
    Richer's legal nuggets.
    1. Law—England—Anecdotes, facetiae,
    satire, etc.
    I. Title
344.2′00207   K184.2

ISBN 0-356-12823-7

Typeset by Clifford-Cooper Ltd,
The Mews, Farnham, Surrey
Printed and bound in Great Britain by
Hazell, Watson & Viney Ltd
A member of the BPCC Group
Aylesbury
Bucks

CONTENTS

INTRODUCTION

Despite the Arthur Daleys among us, the English are essentially a law-abiding people. Lenin said that if they planned to storm a railway station they would all buy platform tickets first. I think this is also the reason why insurance premiums are generally much lower here than, say, in the USA: there are far fewer inflated insurance claims. We have a healthy respect for law and order and our policemen go about their duties unarmed. However, all virtues have their vices and the English generally find talking about money rather distasteful. They are also inclined to accept the status quo and rarely question the statements and claims of banks, building societies, insurance companies and the other great financial institutions, particularly when they are presented as holy writ under impressive logos. Lawyers, on the other hand, have always been held in marked distrust. Shaw said all professions were conspiracies against the laity, a judgement the man on the Clapham omnibus would not fault. The greatest odium has been reserved for lawyers. 'Sue, Grabbit and Run' are only three in a long line of miscreants abhorred by the man in the street who stands shoulder-to-shoulder with Dick the Butcher in *Henry VI Part II* when he advises Jack Cade, the Arthur Scargill of his day: 'The first thing we do, let's kill all the lawyers'.

I like to think that some lawyers have their uses, and hope that from this collection of legal titbits readers may pull out a plum or two which may save them a headache, heartache, money, or all three.

Percy Richer

1

MONEY, MONEY, MONEY

CREDIT CARDS

You go into a travel agency and book a holiday for, say, £2,000. You pay £1,500 in cash on the spot and £500 (since this is your credit limit) on your Access card, Barclaycard, or other credit card. A week before you are due to fly out on holiday the firm shuts up shop and goes bust; you have no tickets, just a receipt. Where do you stand?

You will be pleased to know that if you can't get the money back from the travel firm, the credit card company is legally liable to compensate you in full for the £2,000 you have lost, that is, not only the money paid with the credit card but also the cash. Furthermore the bank concerned has to pay your consequential losses, that is, in legal jargon, 'damages flowing from the breach of contract'. If you can find only more expensive accommodation and have to take a scheduled flight rather than a charter, they have to pay up.

This goes for any purchase of goods or services, such as a secondhand car or double glazing, where a credit card company is involved. This is because the Consumer Credit Act 1974 (Section 75) makes the credit supplier equally liable with the shopkeeper or tour operator for the quality of the goods or services supplied. Incidentally, in the case of travel it's always a good idea to make payments to the tour operator not the travel agent, as banks have sometimes got off the hook by claiming that the travel agent was not the contracting party, but only the agent.

The credit card company can only escape liability in this triangular situation if any one of the following conditions is not met:
1. The cash price for the goods or services must be between £100 and £30,000.

2. The agreement between you and the credit card company must be a commercial agreement — but it always is.

3. Your credit card must have been issued after 1 July 1977. You can see that these are not very onerous conditions.

Of course if you have any reasonable complaints against the double-glazing firm relating to the quality of the work — whether the firm has gone bust or not — the bank has to pay up also.

You can see that the offer of a credit card is one you really can't refuse. Your credit limit may be only £500 but your cover for claims under the Act is unlimited. The sky's the limit. Have you noticed that the banks do not publicize their liability in these matters? No prizes for telling me why they don't. But choke back your sobs for the banks. Remember:

1. This is a great incentive for everybody to have a credit card which in turn brings in interest at an almost usurious rate of 28 per cent per annum — or more.

2. Out of the enormous figure of, for example, 7½ million Barclaycards in circulation, only very few cardholders pursue the banks for compensation — although I assume the number of claims will rise somewhat when this book is published. May the banks forgive me. I hope so. Some of my best friends are bank managers.

However, it is important to remember that what you have just read does *not* apply to goods or services bought on American Express or Diners cards. These are strictly *charge* cards, not *credit* cards. There is a big difference. Only credit-supplying companies such as Access and Barclaycard, and hire-purchase and finance companies are caught by the 1974 Act.

BUYING AND SELLING

You see a sofa priced at £500 in the window of a furniture shop. You go in, agree to buy it and ask for it to be delivered in a couple of weeks' time. You will pay for it on delivery. The day before it is due to be delivered there is an accidental fire at the furniture shop and the sofa is destroyed. You still have to pay the shop the £500 even though all they can give you is a few charred pieces of wood.

The law says that once you have unconditionally agreed to buy anything 'unless a different intention appears ... the property (i.e. the legal ownership) in the goods passes to the buyer when the contract is made, and it is immaterial whether the time of payment or the time of delivery be postponed'.

While you may think this is a little unfair it is only on a par with the situation that arises when you exchange contracts for the purchase of the house. Once you exchange contracts the house is at your risk even though you have not paid for it and if it burns down you still have to complete on the contractual completion date and hand over the money.

There are two ways in which you can safeguard your position with the sofa. Either you can insure it, which is a little bit long winded, or more simply you make it perfectly plain to the shop that you are not going to take legal ownership of the sofa until it is delivered. The key words in the Sale of Goods Act 1979 are 'unless a different intention appears'. All you have to do is to write on the order when you sign it 'legal ownership to pass on delivery'. The shop will then have no claim on you.

By the same token, if you are in business and selling something — say a cash register to a wine bar — and the agreement is for you to be paid within 30 days of delivery, always mark the invoice 'the property in these goods does not pass until payment is made'. This means you will remain the legal owner even though the wine bar goes bust and all the assets are claimed by the Liquidator. You just walk in and take your goods back. But you can't do this without proving 'the different intention', i.e. that the ownership of the goods did not pass when the wine bar gave you the order.

BUYING A CAR
If you buy even a secondhand car it usually involves an

outlay of quite a lot of money, indeed after a house it may be the largest purchase you ever make. The law is therefore very strict with people who misrepresent the condition of cars they sell. The most common practice is for car mileometers to be set back by 10, 20 or even 30 thousand miles so that the vendor can get more money for it. The Trade Descriptions Acts of 1968 and 1972 make it illegal for traders to describe goods and services falsely or display misleadingly low prices. The Institute of Trading Standards Administration has recently estimated that 'clocking' frauds could be costing motorists £250 million per year, and it is no surprise that the courts take the offence of changing the mileage very seriously. In June 1985 three Essex car dealers were each jailed for a year for 'clocking' cars.

What can you do if you buy a car and find later that the mileometer has been set back? All you have to do is contact the trading standards officer of your local council and he will take the necessary action as far as the criminal side is concerned although it might well turn out that the dealer sold the car to you in good faith, thinking the mileage was true when he bought it himself. In this case action can be taken against the person who sold it to him even though he may have been a private seller (the Trade Descriptions Acts normally only apply to transactions in the course of trade or business) and he can be prosecuted.

But there you are — with the car worth half the price you paid for it. How can you get some of your money back? To take the offender to court and sue him, as we all know, can be very time-consuming and expensive. I've news for you: there is a much easier way to get compensation. In whatever court your case is heard the Bench has powers under Section 35 of the Powers of Criminal Courts Act 1973 to make a compensation order against anyone convicted of an offence. The maximum compensation that can be ordered in a magistrates' court is now £2,000 — which should cover most cases nicely. By the way, these compensation orders are not restricted to cars; many relate to other kinds of stolen and unrecovered property.

AUCTIONS
Some very odd things are sold by auction.

LIFE POLICIES
There is an auction firm in the City which specializes in selling reversionary policies. I'll explain. If you take out a life policy, say for £20,000, with an insurance company which guarantees to pay out on your death, you can sell this policy — it is called 'assigning' it — to anybody you like who will collect the cash when you finally go. Now, it's obviously not worth their while paying £20,000 for the policy, but bearing in mind your expectation of life, if you are 70, say, your policy would be worth picking up for about £10,000. I find the whole thing a bit gruesome: it's really investing in death because the sooner you die the more profit is likely to be made by the buyer.

Very often you are asked to assign your life policy to a bank or building society to secure a mortgage on your house, in fact this is what the majority of assignments are for. I find it a bit distasteful that these institutions could benefit if you jumped off Clifton suspension bridge.

Mind you, the French have few inhibitions about investing in death. In the Property for Sale columns in nearly all French newspapers you will see a section headed *Rentes Viagères*. This is for house owners who are prepared to sell their homes in return for a pension the buyer pays them, sometimes with a lump sum, which stops when the seller dies. It is a very thriving business but subject to strict legal controls.

WORKS OF ART
We all know that the famous American painter Jackson Pollock used to create his paintings by riding a bicycle over the canvas to produce the results he wanted. These artefacts are very expensive, costing nowadays very often over £100,000 to buy. You will be pleased to hear that there are quite a number in the Tate Gallery today, to the purchase of which you and I and other taxpayers have contributed. They have jumped in value enormously over the last few

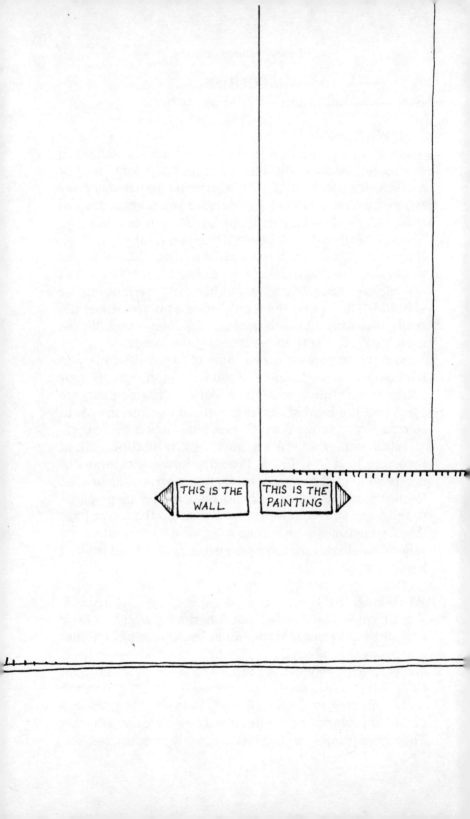

years. I read in *The Times* in 1984 that a painting by a living French artist which was a large piece of canvas painted all over in one shade of blue fetched over £150,000 at Sotheby's. Similarly, in May 1985, as the *Daily Telegraph* reported, 'a huge canvas painted with two vertical bands of colour, dark blue and blue-black, made a new record for the American artist Barnett Newman when it was sold at Sotheby's in New York for £1,169,354'. (I know Dulux is not as cheap as it used to be but I think this is a bit strong.)

While we are on the subject of painting let's spend a moment on Francis Bacon, considered by those who know to be the greatest living English artist. At auction his paintings have been fetching unprecedented prices for a living artist. His speciality is painting portraits of naked men reminiscent of the Elephant Man squatting on a lavatory and screaming their heads off, or what looks like their heads. Mr Bacon also does a nice line in screeching chimpanzees and howling dogs — if you can recognize them.

Bernard Levin (*The Times*, 28 June 1985) estimated that in another 50 years you will be able to pick these masterpieces up at £2 a hundredweight. Meanwhile you'll have to pay around £20,000 to £30,000 a pound if you're really keen to have an elephant man on your drawing room wall, because this is the price these canvases have been puffed up to at recent auctions by enthusiastic collectors and dealers. Mr Bacon is certainly bringing it home.

Of course, we also know all about Tom Keating, the celebrated art faker who died recently. His faked Samuel Palmers fetched record prices at Sotheby's and Christie's in his heyday.

Which brings me to Victorian photographs. For the life of me I have never been able to understand why they fetch such high prices at auctions. A great photograph can always be reproduced from a *negative*, which is the real work of art, and this is a mechanical, not an artistic process. All photographs are literally 'reproductions'. A photograph can be one of a hundred copies and is thus not an original work, like a painting. Does anybody pay thousands for the print of an oil painting? Some exposure called for, I think.

NAPOLEON — BEING THE STORY OF A FAMOUS GENERAL AND HIS PRIVATES

Listen to this. In 1969 Christie's held an auction of what was called the Vignali Collection of Napoleonic relics. Let *The Times* of 30 October 1969 speak for itself:

> This most curious collection including the former emperor's death mask ... specimens of hair from his head, beard and body and *many other odd objects*, was brought back from St Helena by Napoleon's chaplain the Abbé Ange Paul Vignali ... Most curious is a lot described in the catalogue as a *mummified tendon*. It is confirmed by St Denis that he and Vignali took away small pieces of Napoleon's corpse during the autopsy.

Prick up your ears, did I say? The 'mummified tendon' was Christie's delicate euphemism for the great emperor's — er — organ. (The 'great' refers to the emperor, by the way.) I am not having you on. I am given to treating such private matters with the seriousness they deserve and checked my references with Mr Mark Wrey, Christie's Public Relations Officer, who confirmed that mine was not the first enquiry. But he said that there was some doubt as to what it was. And *whose* it was if that was *what* it was.

Oh, yes, the auction. Well, the auctioneer didn't seem to have a feeling for his subject and it was all a bit of a cock-up one way or another, since the main bidder, a Mr Bruce Gimelson of Fort Washington, Pennsylvania, got quite excited and seemed to be bidding against himself most of the time. Anyway, the collection failed to reach its reserve and at £17,000 was 'bought in', that is withdrawn — a case of auction interruptus, as you might say. Napoleon was a sensible chap and would have probably taken a detached view of the whole affair.

I mention all these unusual auction lots because you must take care if you buy or, for that matter, *sell* anything at auction. So much has been written about auctions that

Money, Money, Money

I will keep the rest brief. Just some words of warning:

1. Never pick your nose at an auction or you may find you have bought a grand piano. The auctioneer is entitled to take any reasonable signal as a bid.

2. The auctioneer is always acting for the seller and owes no duty of care to the buyer except in special circumstances.

3. He very often gives no guarantee as to the provenance (which really means genuineness) of the lots he sells. That is, he only sticks his neck out and says the painting is by Rembrandt if this is absolutely incontrovertible. But what does 'absolutely' mean? Art experts, just as much as any other experts, often disagree among themselves, and they are very often as gullible as the man in the street — sometimes more so. Even Lord Dacre, formerly Hugh Trevor-Roper, the eminent Oxford historian, gave an authoritative opinion that the forged Hitler diaries were on the level.

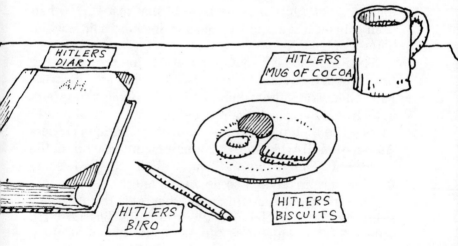

4. If you are selling (and sometimes buying) beware the 'Ring' as much as Alice's Jabberwock ('the jaws that bite, the claws that catch'). The Ring operates very simply: some bidders, mainly dealers, get together before the sale and agree that one of their number will buy a lot cheaply (the others not bidding against him). Afterwards they hold a select private auction among themselves in the local hotel, even on the beach, as was the case which the police rumbled in the 1970s, and the losers all take a cut. The winner gets the piece he wants at a knock-down price. This secondary auction is called 'the knockout'. The division of the proceeds is called 'the settlement'.

Of course, it's all strictly illegal, for in 1927 Parliament passed the Auctions (Bidding Agreements) Act, prohibiting all this. Sounds very impressive, doesn't it? But only one prosecution under it came to court in the next 40 years. In that time, of course, unscrupulous dealers made hay. Then, in the 1960s the National Gallery bought a painting for £150,000. Only it came to light that just £2,700 had been paid for it at a country house in Somerset a little while before.

The Ring had also operated in 1964 after the sale of the furniture of Captain E.G. Spencer-Churchill at Northwick Park, Gloucestershire, when *The Sunday Times* (bless 'em) got a friend to tape all the proceedings at the local pub in secret. The then president of the British Antique Dealers Association (BADA) and 13 council members who, in the words of *The Sunday Times*, 'had all had some involvement', resigned some weeks later.

So Parliament brought in another Act, the Auctions (Bidding Agreements) Act 1969: but this has no teeth either. BADA, which has 450 members, several of them quite prestigious, now tries to control the activities of its members but it's a big headache for them. Responsible dealers blame the Government, as I do, for not taking a strong line with the offenders. As Hugh Leggatt, of the very grand firm of fine art dealers, Leggatt Brothers, said in a letter to *The Times* concerning a Queen Anne bookcase bought by the Ring not so long ago: 'I just wonder whether the present scandal is going to be another case of *plus ça change, plus c'est la même chose'*. Meantime, the ring cycle goes on playing music to the ears of unscrupulous dealers who continue to defy the law at the expense of the public.

To sum up, *be careful* if you sell anything remotely valuable at an auction, whether it is a house, commode, or just a dusty picture left to you by your great aunt. At least make the auctioneer put a realistic reserve price on it. Or better still, shop around and get two or three independent valuations. You can be gypped rotten.

This can also happen if you are *buying* something and incur the wrath of the Ring. They will then bid you up and up and in the heat of the moment you may find yourself paying twice as much as the lot is worth. Hugh Leggatt has no illusions about his business. 'We are only one remove from barrow boys', he admits (*Sunday Telegraph*, 14 July 1985).

AUCTIONEERS' LIABILITY
You are strapped for money, so you persuade your wife to let you put her diamond necklace into an auction. Despite very stringent security measures the necklace is stolen while on display in the middle of the auction company's viewing gallery. The auctioneers are clearly to blame. Or are they?

These were the facts in Spriggs v. Sotheby (1984), only it wasn't a necklace, just a single diamond. Sotheby's, however, got off the hook and paid no compensation to Mr Spriggs. They relied on the small print in an exclusion clause on the back of the sale form signed by Mr Spriggs. He had declined an offer by Sotheby's to insure the diamond for an extra charge, and the auctioneers had exempted themselves from any liability for loss. Which only goes to show that you must always read the small print, however boring or arduous this may be. And if it's not clear, *always ask*.

Although this case was reported only in 1984, Mr Spriggs signed the sale form before the Unfair Contract Terms Act of

1977 was passed. This Act changed the law somewhat, inasmuch as Sotheby's would now have to satisfy the court that the exclusion clause had been 'reasonable'. But it seems that they would still have won the case.

DEBTS

WHAT'S HE TALKING ABOUT? I DON'T OWE HIM A PENNY

If someone writes to you saying that you owe them money, and you don't, reply at once denying their claim. And look into the matter very carefully to make sure you are not liable in any way.

A butcher client of mine had to pay over £10,000 to a woman who tripped up outside his shop because he ignored all her letters and a summons, and put in no defence at court. He thought the pavement outside his shop belonged to the council. In fact he owned the forecourt himself and *was* liable. The irony is that he would have been fully covered under his insurance policy if he had claimed on it straight away.

If he had come to see me sooner I could have dealt with it under the public liability section of his policy within the insurance company's very strict time limits and he need not have paid a penny. As it was, he had to mortgage his house to pay off the debt. A lot of people own part of the pavement outside their houses or shops. So if you do, watch no-one trips up on it.

Note Even if you are in no way liable, always repudiate in writing a claim made against you without foundation — immediately — and keep a copy of your letter. Send the original by recorded delivery. Better still, see a solicitor. Silence may be taken as an admission of the allegation, and this may be costly and time-consuming to disprove later.

INSURANCE

You own a cottage in the country and keep it insured for the full cost of reinstatement, say £14,000. You have it on the market, though, for just £4,500 because this is the price at which cottages like yours are changing hands. The cottage burns down; it is agreed that it will cost about £9,000 to reinstate it. How much will you get from the insurance company? You will get £4,500 *less* the value of the land. The site is worth £1,500, so you end up with just £3,000. This is because a contract of house or car insurance, etc. is a contract of indemnity, and consequently it will only cover your *actual loss* up to the limit of your policy, no matter how much your cover. Of course, if the property had been with agents to sell at a higher price, the insurance company would have shelled out that much more. These were the facts in the case of Leppard v. Excess Insurance Co. Ltd in 1979, decided in the Court of Appeal. You can't win, can you?

STOLEN GOODS

IT FELL OFF THE BACK OF A LORRY, GUV
You can get up to 14 years for buying stolen goods knowingly. An innocent buyer won't get convicted, of course, but he can be made to hand the goods back to the true owner. However, there are two important exceptions when he can keep them. First, if you are a private individual (i.e. not a trader who is deemed to be more conversant with the ways of this wicked world) and you buy a motor car which is being bought on hire purchase and not yet paid for, you are protected by the Hire Purchase Act 1964. Provided you didn't know about the hire purchase you can keep it.

The second is a more curious exception applying to all stolen goods. If they are sold in any shop in the City of London or in any properly constituted open market (except, strangely enough, in Wales) between the hours of sunrise and sunset the original owner cannot claim them back and you can keep them. This is the ancient rule of 'market overt' going back to the sixteenth century.

Be very careful if you buy anything in Golden Lane, EC1, though. In my *A to Z* only half appears to be within the City proper — make sure you go to the right half.

DRUNK BUT NOT DISORDERLY

You are in a pub or nightclub getting very, very sloshed. You are wearing an old suede jacket with grease spots on it which you had been thinking of replacing. A man comes up to you with a new suede jacket which seems to fit the bill at a reasonable price. He is a leather dealer and it's all above board. You agree to buy it for, say, £100 and arrange for the dealer to bring it to your office in the morning to collect the money. By this time you are so newt-like that you don't know what you are doing. The dealer turns up with the jacket the next day but you don't remember a thing although your mates told you when you had sobered up what you had done. Your wife tells you you are a fool and she needs the money for housekeeping.

Do you have to pay up and take the jacket? You do. If you had agreed, while drunk, to buy the QE2 or London Bridge, or even a diamond necklace, you wouldn't be held to it. But in these circumstances the jacket is considered to be 'a necessary'. The Sale of Goods Act 1979 states specifically '... where necessaries are sold and delivered to an infant or minor, or to a person who by reason of mental incapacity or *drunkenness* is incompetent to contract, he must pay a reasonable price therefor. Necessaries ... means goods suitable to the condition in life of such infant or minor or other person, *and to his actual requirements at the time of sale and delivery.*'

The vital words are in italics. You've had it. And curiously, as you see, children and lunatics also have to pay up (they don't have to be drunk, of course, for the contract to be legal and enforceable).

Shocked! I'm not surprised. Never give kids and lunatics credit: you may not get the cash if the goods aren't 'necessaries'. By the way, this applies not only to suede jackets and suchlike but also to false teeth, as the Judge ruled in the case of Johnston v. Powell. I think this is called putting teeth into the law.

2

THE LEX OF SEX

The thing that takes up the least amount of time
and causes the most amount of trouble is sex.

John Barrymore

I never realized you could have so much fun
without laughing.

Woody Allen

'Love between man and woman ... consumes energy and
wastes time. On the other hand, love of the party, and the
chairman ... takes no time at all and is in itself a powerful
tonic.' No, this is not an extract from the Conservative or
Labour Party manifesto, as you might easily have thought,
and not the reason why Denis Thatcher and Neil Kinnock
always look so full of vitality. It is from the *Peking Workers
Daily* and the chairman referred to was 'speedy' Mao Tse
Tung. In China, as in the world of Islam, sex is taken
seriously.

Certainly in Riyadh if you have a bit on the side you're
liable to get your hand cut off, if not worse. I ask you —
is it worth it? As Lord Chesterfield is reputed to have said
'the pleasure is momentary, the position ridiculous, and
the expense damnable'.

For all that, the general view seems to be 'damn the
expense'. Indeed, Dr Dennis Lincoln of the Medical
Research Council's Reproductive Biology Unit — and he
should know — told the British Association on 29 August
1985 that we are 10,000 times more sexually prolific than
rabbits and do it 1,000 million times a year. And that's just
in Britain alone. Three million times a day. God knows
what goes on abroad.

So if you still feel it's one of life's pleasures not to be
lightly dismissed you should know where you stand. What

is your position as regards sex? I'll rephrase that: under the laws of this country what may you do, mustn't you do, and shouldn't you do? I shall tell you.

SEX AND MARRIAGE: BEFORE, AFTER AND OUTSIDE
Here are some answers to a lot of unspoken questions.

BEFORE (Pre-marital sex)
Virginity. Neither party to a marriage has to be a virgin, nor disclose his or her sexual past to the other.
VD. If either party has venereal disease in a communicable form, the marriage will be voidable and the other spouse can petition for a decree of nullity within three years of the marriage, only if he or she was not aware of the facts at the time of the marriage — but not *after* three years.
Pregnancy. If the wife was at the time of marriage pregnant by someone other than her husband and her husband did not know this, the same proceedings may be taken. If the husband had made *another* woman pregnant, the wife unfortunately cannot complain — legally, that is, except in the enlightened courts of New Zealand. In that country the wife can have the marriage made null and void on those grounds.
Accepting the position. If the parties were aware of pregnancy or venereal disease *before* the marriage and still went ahead accepting the position, they are said to 'approbate' the marriage and will be unable to get a decree of nullity. If they learn about it *after* the marriage but not from the offending party, this could amount to unreasonable behaviour and constitute grounds for divorce. It it is disclosed by one partner to the other, the latter has the option of approbating the marriage or taking proceedings.

AFTER (sex in marriage)
Consummation. If you get married you have to consummate the marriage (just once is enough), otherwise your partner can have the marriage set aside. What does 'consummation' mean? According to the *Oxford English*

Dictionary it means 'the completing of marriage by sexual intercourse'. The word was used in this way as long ago as 1540. But this only tells half the story. As you would expect, the *legal* definition goes into the subject with much more thrust, and I'm afraid we're going to get rather clinical here.

Depth of penetration. The man's penis must penetrate the woman's vagina quite a bit (more than that required to prove rape) if not all the way. In an unhappy case (D-e v. A-g 1845) the wife's sexual organs were malformed (her vagina was a sort of cul-de-sac) and she fell short of permitting complete coitus. When this happens, the Judge declared rather luridly, 'almost of necessity disgust is generated, and the probable consequences of other connections' (presumably meaning adultery, or worse) 'with men of ordinary self-control become almost certain. No man ought to be reduced to this state of ... temptation, and therefore I should hold the marriage void.'

Duration of penetration. Not only must the penis enter the vagina to a reasonable depth: it must stay there a reasonable time. If it doesn't, in the eyes of the law 'ordinary or complete' intercourse is not established, particularly if there is no emission of semen (W. v. W. 1967). But what is reasonable? It all depends on the circumstances.

No penetration but impregnation. What if the husband doesn't penetrate his wife at all but as a result of ejaculations outside, a child is born (by what is called fecundation ab extra)? These were the facts in the case of Clarke v. Clarke in 1943. The wife had petitioned for divorce because of Mr Clarke's adultery, who cross-petitioned for a decree of nullity, claiming the marriage had never been consummated. He succeeded.

AIH/AID. Similarly if the wife is artificially inseminated by her husband's or a donor's semen, or a mixture of both, there is no consummation.

Penetration but no orgasm. What if the husband effects an erection and a full penetration of the wife but is unable to ejaculate (i.e. have an orgasm), as was the case

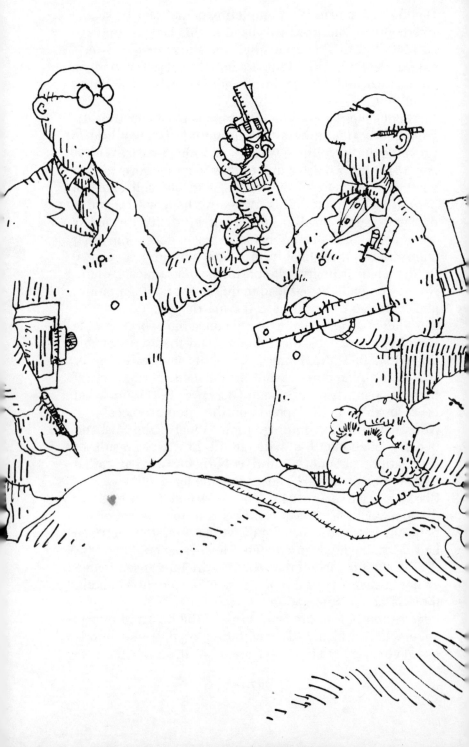

in R. v. R. in 1952? The marriage is deemed to be consummated. Neither party is legally entitled to an orgasm.

False vaginas, etc. Can a marriage be consummated with a vagina which is wholly artificial, or an artificial penis, or a vibrator? No, it can't.

No conception. Does a child have to be conceived as a result of the copulation? No, it doesn't. You can't ask for a decree of nullity just because you can't have children. You have consummated the marriage if you meet the other conditions.

French letters. If no semen is deposited in the vagina by the use of a sheath, or the wife uses a contraceptive device, what then? Well, until 1948 this was deemed to be non-consummation, surprisingly enough. Then in the case of Baxter v. Baxter the previous decisions were reversed.

Coitus interruptus. Since this is also a form of contraception the same reasoning applies. It is not by itself non-consummation but may be grounds for divorce for what used to be known as cruelty and now constitutes unreasonable behaviour.

Agreement not to consummate. What if the parties to a marriage agree beforehand not to consummate it (Brodie v. Brodie 1917)? Such an agreement is against public policy and invalid. If the husband or wife reneges on the 'agreement' once they are married and wants out, a decree of nullity will be given if there has been no consummation. But if they wish to abide by the 'agreement', which has no force in law, they are said to 'approbate' the marriage, that is, accept the position, since the agreement has become a properly acceptable arrangement reached *after* the marriage, which is quite in order (Scott v. Scott 1959). Very often elderly people marry with no desire for, or expectation of, sex. If you are one of these you can nevertheless petition for a decree of nullity for non-consummation (provided you haven't 'approbated' the marriage), though I find this a bit hard on the other party.

Sex before marriage. Say you had satisfactory sex before you got married but then didn't meet the requirements

afterwards. Could you claim you had consummated the
marriage in anticipation? No, you couldn't.

EVERYDAY SEX IN MARRIAGE
Rape. Each partner owes the other a duty to have
reasonable sex, that is reasonable in quantity and quality.
But we still have the strange anomaly of the wife who is
expected to submit to her husband even if he takes her by
force. A husband simply cannot be guilty of raping his
wife. (It is different in Scotland. See page 39.) The most
he can be charged with is indecent assault. This immunity
persists even if the parties are living apart without a decree
nisi or a court order for judicial separation.
Sex within reason. If either party denies sex to the other
without good reason or insists on having it in a way
repugnant to the other — such as a man insisting on the
use of a contraceptive knowing that his wife wanted to have
a child — this would constitute unreasonable behaviour.
Other forms of such behaviour in the sexual context could
be the practice of coitus interruptus (Holborn v. Holborn
1947), the carrying out of sterilization on the husband
without good medical reason and without the wife's
consent, and transvestism of the husband. Inability to
perform (impotence) is not itself cruelty though it may be
the principal factor in the breakdown of a marriage.
Swinging sex. Experimenting with one's partner is quite
common, as many have witnessed over the centuries:
'Certainly nothing is unnatural that is not physically
impossible' (Sheridan, *The Critic*), 'Sexuality is the
lyricism of the masses' (Baudelaire), 'The degree and kind
of a man's sexuality reach up into the ultimate pinnacle
of his spirit' (Nietzsche). 'Is sex dirty?' Woody Allen was
asked. 'Only if you do it right,' he replied. And Groucho
Marx, asked at the end of a very long life whether he would
live his life over again without any changes, thought for
a moment and said: 'I'd try a few new positions.'

The law has no objection to any out-of-the-ordinary
sexual practices between spouses (provided they're agreed
between them, otherwise unreasonable behaviour may

result) and this can take in all kinds of 'deviations' (I put these words in quotes because one man's deviations may be another person's norm), such as sex in the mouth (fellatio), licking the vagina (cunnilingus), masturbation, dressing up, or even wife-swopping. There is nothing wrong, legally, with any of this behaviour. (Or medically: an eminent physician, Dr Rob Buckman, has categorically confirmed that oral sex does not damage your health. All it can possibly damage, he says, is your conversation.)

Buggery. There is one curious exception to the above. While buggery is not a criminal offence in Great Britain between consenting males in private over the age of 21 (it is in Northern Ireland), it still is a crime between a man and a *woman*, including married partners, and punishable with imprisonment for life. In 1971 a Mr Harris got 18 months for it. Now, here's a strange situation. If a wife agrees to sodomy by the husband (a criminal offence, as I said) she cannot afterwards file for divorce because of the fact of sodomy, since she consented to it and condoned it. This happened to a Mrs Hampton in 1959 and her petition was refused by Lord Justice Hodson. Buggery, by the way, consists in sexual intercourse *per anum* (that is, up the back passage) by a man with another man or a woman, or with an animal (up the back or front passage). It is a wider offence than 'sodomy' which only covers so-called unnatural intercourse between human beings.)

Lesbianism. Lesbianism (homosexual acts between women) is not usually a criminal offence. The exceptions are where there is no consent by one of the parties, where-upon the act becomes an indecent assault. No consent can be given by a girl under the age of 16, nor by a mental defective. You will note I used the word 'homosexual' in connection with lesbians. It's a common mistake to think that 'homosexuals' are just *men* indulging in sex acts with each other. If you look the word up in your dictionary you will see that a *homosexual* is 'a person who is sexually attracted to members of the same sex' as distinct from a *heterosexual* who is 'a person sexually attracted to the opposite sex'. The misconception probably arose because *homo* means 'man' in Latin, whereas the 'homo' part of homosexual comes from the Greek word meaning 'the same'. So a woman who is a lesbian is a female homosexual. The word 'gay' similarly covers both men and women homosexuals.

If you happen to swing both ways ('AC/DC'), you are *bisexual.*

You can't get a decree of nullity just because your partner is a homosexual or bisexual but it could possibly constitute unreasonable behaviour for a divorce petition.

I should say a word here about the phrase 'unreasonable behaviour', which, although often used even in legal circles, is inaccurate. What it actually means is behaviour which would make it unreasonable to expect one partner to continue living with the other. It follows that this behaviour will usually be unreasonable itself — but not always. For example, if a wife reports her husband to the police for cruelty to the kids when she discovers marks on them after they have been left with him for the evening, and it transpires that he is not to blame, although her behaviour in reporting him may be reasonable, it may also make it unreasonable to expect the husband to continue to live with her. This also applies when someone can't help his behaviour, for example when reduced to imbecility by illness.

The inferior position of women. If you're a woman you may well think marriage and slavery have a lot in common. Your position in society and in the eyes of the law tends to make you a second-class citizen. A fairly typical male view of women is summed up by the man who, seeing a sign outside a fish and chip shop, 'Cleanliness, economy, and civility, always hot and ready', remarked 'The motto of the perfect wife'. *Kinder, Kirche, Küche,* no less. (Children, church and kitchen). Here are some anomalies:

The oversexed man. In marriage you may have to submit to sex by force, wherever and whenever your husband wants it. You may get him for the minor offence of assault but you would have to bring a private prosecution. The male dominated legislature, judiciary and executive — Parliament, the Judges, and the police — seem to think that if you have slept with your husband before being married to him, as the chances are you have, it wouldn't be a crime for him to have his way with you when you aren't in the mood. Indeed, in one nullity case based on the wife's lack of interest the Judge thought it might have been better if the husband had used some 'gentle violence' instead of taking his wife's objections at their face value! (G. v. G. 1924).

The undersexed man. In other ways also the law has historically catered for the sexual needs of the husband rather than the wife and this bias persists today. If you are frigid by nature because of a fear of bearing a child, your husband can divorce you (P.[D] v. P. [J] 1965). But your man won't be condemned if he's undersexed or uninterested (B. [L] v. B. [R] 1965) and you may not get your divorce, even though your health suffers. Again, the Court of Appeal refused to nullify the marriage of a Mrs Potter on the grounds of non-consummation by her husband who had suffered a 'loss of ardour' after Mrs Potter underwent an operation to enable the marriage to be consummated. The Bench felt Mr Potter couldn't help himself.

If you live with a man but not in wedlock you cannot legally make him support you. And if the relationship breaks up while he is supporting you, you can't get a maintenance order against him. But if he *dies* while supporting you, partly or wholly, you can claim reasonable provision from his estate, even though you had only been living together for a short time. This gives you almost the same rights as a wife. Yet if you marry him after living together for several years and the marriage ends in divorce, the period spent living together does not count when calculating the support to which you may be entitled (Campbell v. Campbell 1976).

Finally, as far as both sexes are concerned, I find it sad that in the courts reference is rarely made to 'making love' — sex being a supreme act of love. The 55 clauses of the

Matrimonial Causes Act 1973, which legislates on almost all matrimonial problems, make no mention of the words 'love' and 'affection'. Nor could I find these words in this context in either Halsbury's Laws (the authoritative statement of all English law) or in the four thousand pages of Rayden on Divorce (the lawyer's bible on the subject). That consummation should depend on how many inches a woman is penetrated, reducing the sex act to a mechanical process and bringing it almost within the scope of the Weights and Measures Office, seems to me a defilement of what can and should be one of the greatest acts of union to which we can aspire. I look forward to the day when Judges will ask not only 'How far did it go in?' but 'When he tried to make love to you was he caring and considerate? Was he trying to show his love for you? If he was, he has no case to answer.'

SEX OUTSIDE THE MARRIAGE (adultery)

> The pleasures of childhood are nothing
> compared to the joys of adultery.
>
> Schoolboy's essay

> *What men call gallantry, and gods adultery,*
> *Is much more common where the climate's sultry.*
>
> Lord Byron, *Don Juan*

What does 'adultery' mean? Adultery is sex with consent between persons one of whom is, or both of whom are, married, but not to each other. Adultery is thus not committed by a woman who is raped, but it is by the rapist if he is married. Full penetration by the penis of the vagina is not essential, though there must be some entry, which need only be very brief. The criteria are much less strict than those required to prove consummation (see pages 26-29). It was even held in 1938 that a Mrs Thompson who was found to be a virgin after an alleged act of adultery did in fact transgress. But when a Mr Sapsford in 1954 tried to gain entry without success there was no adultery. And masturbation by one partner of the other does not amount to adultery either. Neither is artificial insemination of the wife by a donor who is not her husband, as there is no penetration.

If a wife is seduced by a man who has poured drink into her, or given her drugs, against her will, she does not commit adultery. But if she agrees to drink with a man who is not her husband and sleeps with him after getting so sloshed that she has no idea of what is happening, she does (Goshawk v. Goshawk 1965).

There is no such thing as adultery by rape. A Mrs Clarkson was raped in 1930 and even though she gave birth to a child as a result, her husband couldn't get a divorce for adultery because she didn't consent to have sex with the rapist.

It is up to the spouse who alleges the adultery (the 'petitioner') to prove it; the other partner is presumed innocent until proved guilty. Most cases of adultery are admitted by the spouse who has side-stepped (the 'respondent'). But curiously the third party — the 'other' man or woman (the 'co-respondent') — if married to someone else may not be found to have committed adultery on the strength of this alone.

Where there is no confession there must be some evidence to persuade the Judge that adultery took place. This doesn't have to be a photograph of the couple in bed, despite what you see in films. If proof is given of inclination and opportunity, that's enough. When a Mr Blum booked a double room and went there with a woman who was not his wife, his protestations of innocence were not accepted by the court in 1963 and Mrs Blum got her divorce. And in 1919 a Mrs Jolly was judged to have committed adultery (it's funny that we still speak of 'committing' adultery as though it's a criminal offence. We don't speak of 'committing' matrimony. Well, at least, not most of us) even though she was still *virgo intacta*, because opportunity and inclination were obvious, and the judge drew his own conclusions, partial penetration being enough to prove adultery.

If you get VD from another person while married this is evidence of adultery.

If the wife gives birth to a child which is not her husband's this is likewise evidence of adultery, but of course it must be proved. Blood tests can offer firm proof that a husband is not the father of a child, and they can also indicate what proportion of the male population could be the father. But only the new DNA tests can provide conclusive evidence that a man is the father of a child ... except when the father is a twin!

Near misses (i.e. no penetration). Masturbation, fellatio and cunnilingus are grounds for divorce ('unreasonable behaviour') if carried out with someone to whom you're not married. So also, for that matter, are kissing or flirting. But these are always considered in the context of the particular marriage. There is no hard and fast rule (Ash v. Ash 1971).

PROSTITUTES

THE CUSTOMER ALWAYS COMES FIRST

If a man frequents a lady of the night and agrees to pay for her services she cannot sue for the agreed price and he cannot recover his money if she doesn't perform or doesn't come up to scratch. But if he has paid her before the promised act, whether it is consummated or not, he mustn't grab the money and walk off with it. That would be theft.

It is a very serious criminal offence for someone to live off the earnings of prostitution (except the prostitute, of course, since prostitution itself is not a crime). This includes people who supply such ladies and gentlemen with the tools of their trade. In an old case a firm that hired an expensive carriage to a known prostitute could not recover their hire charges.

And if you let a flat to a prostitute knowing that she carries on her profession there she needn't pay you a penny. But if you let the same flat to her and you know that she pays you a rent entirely out of income from prostitution *elsewhere* you are strangely OK because, as an enlightened Judge ruled as long ago as 1826, even 'persons of that description must have a place to lay their heads' (but not their clients, of course).

PROSTITUTES AND INCOME TAX

> The difference between paying for sex, and
> not paying, is that when you don't pay it's
> always much more expensive.
>
> Anon.

Prostitution itself is not a crime. But the law comes down very hard on its by-products such as soliciting, procuring, pimping, and running a brothel. However, while it is a serious criminal offence for someone to live off the earnings of prostitution, the Chancellor of the Exchequer has no inhibitions in swelling his coffers by demanding and collecting income tax from prostitutes. They are expected to fill in their tax returns and pay income tax just like solicitors and doctors and other self-employed professionals.

The taxman is quite businesslike about it and if he gets wind of a prostitute's earnings from sexual service he will assess her for tax, and if need be *estimate* the tax he thinks she should pay, under Schedule D, since she is recognized in the eyes of the law as practising a rewarding profession. I think even the relentless inspectors of the Inland Revenue have the grace and diplomacy to consider her business activities a 'profession' and not a 'trade', as did George Bernard Shaw in *Mrs Warren's Profession*.

My views are reinforced by the legally accepted definition of the word 'profession' which 'involves the idea of an occupation requiring either purely intellectual skill, or *manual* skill controlled by the intellectual skill of the operator' (e.g. teacher, solicitor or surgeon). Of course, if a prostitute decides to ride her bicycle, so to speak, without using her hands, she may find this counter-productive. Almost like putting the ball in her own goal, if I may mix a metaphor, although the referee in the form of the taxman, to be fair, probably won't mark her card. In any event the tax rules for trades and professions are virtually identical.

Cynthia Payne, the Streatham madam who put luncheon vouchers on the map while catering for the appetites of her distinguished clientele, but who was somewhat remiss in declaring her earnings, told me that the Inland Revenue had assessed her for £100,000 in back tax, as they rather ambiguously called it.

The good news for these professional ladies (and gentlemen) is that, in common with all others in gainful self-employment, they can set off against their income all the expenses 'incurred wholly and exclusively' for the purpose of their vocation. Thus they can claim as tax-deductible the cost of maintaining their establishments (provided they don't just sleep there but get on with the job) and personnel and, depending on their various special interests, the cost of the appropriate tools of their trade, or should I say paraphernalia of their profession.

I don't think we'll go into any more detail at this point but it's nice to know the Inland Revenue gives prostitutes a measure of relief (yes, that's the technical term) which goes some way to balance the other kind of relief they give their clients. Mind you, I don't say the taxman feels he should bend over backwards to do this: it's a statutory obligation on his part and if you're really interested you can read all about it in Section 130 of the Income and Corporation Taxes Act 1970.

RAPE

HARD CASES MAKE BAD LAW
A New Zealander by the name of Kaitamaki was in bed with the lady of his choice engaged in what a popular satirical magazine calls Ugandan discussions. Half way through, the lady while, in the language of the law, being 'penetrated' told K. she wanted to break off the discussion but K., no doubt motivated by Magnus Magnusson, said 'I've started, so I'll finish'. He went all the way.

The case also went all the way — to the Privy Council, the highest court in the Commonwealth, who had to decide in October 1984 whether K. had any defence to a charge of rape. Five eminent Judges (Lord Scarman, Sir George Baker, the Master of the Rolls, and their learned brethren) all ruled he hadn't. (K. should have been told, of course, that it wouldn't stand up in court.) Their exact words were 'for the purposes of rape, intercourse is a continuing act so that if (at *any* stage after penetration and before withdrawal) the lady was not consenting, and K. knew this, K. was guilty of rape if he continued the intercourse'. Not very cost-efficient for poor old K., of course, who paid for a few minutes of extra excitement with as many years behind bars.

This judgement has interesting consequences for married couples in Scotland. In England there is no offence of rape between man and wife, unless they are in effect separated, as, for example, by a court order. If a man subjects his wife to a sexual attack she is deemed to consent to intercourse by virtue of her married state. It is what is called an 'attribute of consortium'. Only if he wilfully harms her can he be had up for the crime of assault.

In Scotland it is quite different. The Crown Office in Edinburgh (the equivalent of the Department of the DPP down south) tells me that in a case as recent as August 1984 Lord Cameron held that one John William Paxton did in fact rape his wife and was duly convicted. Take heed, all ye caber-tossers north of the border. If your wife wants a holiday from you for five years or longer, she can entice you into a Ugandan situation and then suggest you scarper. And if you don't you may find yourself with Mr Kaitamaki as a neighbour. Don't whinge; it may be less macho, but it is a good deal safer to let your world end not with a bang, as T.S. Eliot put it, but with a whimper.

RAPE AND PATERNITY

Is a boy under the age of 14 capable of having sexual relations in the eyes of the law? Well, on the one hand he isn't, but on the other hand he is. There is an irrefutable presumption in *criminal* law that a boy under the age of 14 can never be guilty of rape as he is not able to have sexual intercourse. But in *civil* law he is. In L. v. K. in 1985 it was held that this presumption (i.e. that a boy under 14 could not have sexual relations) could have no application in affiliation proceedings (paternity suits). In this particular case there was corroboration that the mother of the baby had had intercourse with a boy aged 13 whom the court concluded was the father. The Judge said paternity was a matter of 'impregnation'. Rape was a matter of 'penetration', and you could have one without the other. You find this hard to follow? What if the boy had *raped* the woman and so impregnated her? There's a teaser for the Bench.

HOMOSEXUALITY

I find it a paradox that while lesbianism — with one exception given below — has never been specifically outlawed in the UK (in 1921 the House of Lords rejected a Bill to make lesbianism a criminal offence), male homosexuality has been considered a criminal activity for centuries. In was the ruin of Oscar Wilde as relatively recently as 1895 when he was sent to prison for two years, and although one of the most successful playwrights of his time, became bankrupt and died neglected in Paris. But he was lucky. If he had lived some 40 years earlier he could have been sent to the gallows as it was then still a crime punishable by death.

However, times have changed and we have all become more tolerant. Nowadays, since the Sexual Offences Act 1967, homosexual behaviour between two consenting men (not more) is lawful if both are over 21, neither is mentally defective, and it's done in private. With one major exception. You can still get up to two years' imprisonment and a dishonourable discharge if you're in the armed forces or the merchant navy. You will be had up for 'buggery' or 'gross indecency' if you do it on a UK merchant ship (you're OK if you're working on a deep-sea oil rig, strangely enough), or for 'disgraceful conduct of an indecent or unnatural kind' if you do it, or prepare 'to commit an offence' (i.e. by talking about it) in the Army, Navy and Air Force. And this applies to lesbians as well.

Now I find all this rather contradictory. The Royal Navy, without any disparagement of the sterling fighting qualities of the members of the senior service, has been associated in the minds of the public for years with homosexual, or at least bisexual practices. Winston Churchill summed it up unkindly as the home of 'rum, bum and the lash'. Only a year or two back half the crew of the Royal Yacht *Britannia* were dismissed for buggering about with each other. In his biography of Lord Mountbatten (*Mountbatten*, Collins 1985, p.51) Philip Ziegler wrote that 'to be caught red-handed was the end of one's career; even to be the subject of rumour was an impediment to promotion' but he also quotes Lord Mountbatten, on being told that his naval servant was homosexual, as replying: 'Of course. All the best valets are.'

The reasons for the alleged prevalence of homosexuality in the Navy are not hard to find. Away from their wives and the hospitality of other companions on shore leaves for several months at a time, sailors perhaps tend to strike up closer friendships with their 'oppos' than in the junior services. This surely goes for their officers too, but it seems they benefit from Nelson's blind eye.

Well, why not? Some of the greatest figures in history had the same inclinations. Socrates had 'wild Alcibiades'; Alexander the Great, Julius Caesar, Plutarch, Leonardo da Vinci and Michaelangelo all seem to have been bisexual. Sappho, probably the poetess of all time, gave the name of her home (the island of Lesbos) to her practices, now called 'lesbian'. Our own King Edward II had Gaveston, according to Christopher Marlowe.

In America the general incidence of homosexual behaviour for white males was given as follows in the classic scientific study, Kinsey's *Sexual Behaviour in the Human Male*:

1. 37 per cent had at least one overt homosexual experience between the onset of adolescence and old age.

2. 10 per cent were predominantly homosexual for at least three years between the ages of 16 and 55.

3. 4 per cent were solely homosexual after the onset of adolescence.

4. 18 per cent of all males have as much homosexual as heterosexual experience in their development.

There is no reason to think that the figures are any different in the UK although I am told by the Gay Rights Movement that the generally accepted statistic is that one man in five is exclusively gay, predominantly gay or gay 'on a part-time basis'.

Many spy scandals this century have involved homosexual behaviour. Burgess and Maclean, Vassall and Blunt are names which spring to mind. The Ministry of Defence has given as one of the chief reasons for maintaining its uncompromising attitude towards homosexuals in the forces its concern that they may be liable to blackmail and thus likely to be a security risk.

While we're on the subject, the scale of penalties for illegal homosexual acts is most odd. A youth of 18 who commits such an act with a boy of 15 is theoretically liable to imprisonment for life. If the accused is over 21 and his partner between 16 and 21 — even though there was consent, he can get five years. And while indecent assault on a woman can bring a maximum of two years the same offence on a man can bring 10 years. Hardly logical.

This is no doubt partly the reason why in October 1985 the Labour Party Conference passed a motion which would have the effect of lowering the homosexual age of consent to 16. (Did you know, by the way, that until 1929 the legal age for marriage was 12? It was increased in that year to 16 by the Marriage Act to bring it into line with the age of consent for girls, which was then — and still is — 16.)

Be it said that the age of consent for homosexuals differs widely from country to country. In Italy, Norway and Portugal there are no special restrictions whatsoever, while in Cyprus, Spain, Romania, the USSR and the Republic of Ireland it's completely illegal. In between, the age of consent varies from 10 years (Hungary) to 21 (UK). In Switzerland, that bastion of the bourgeoisie (where women didn't get the vote until 1971), the age is surprisingly liberally set at 16. And in Bulgaria, where it all seemingly started (the word 'bugger' is derived from 'Bulgar') the age is 21. Finally, if you do get caught engaged in unlawful gay sex you cannot be prosecuted for it more than 12 months after the act unless the offence was with a boy aged under 16, or if your partner (of any age) did not consent to the act.

VENEREAL DISEASE

The English have always taken a robust view of venereal disease which is nowadays euphemistically known as a social disease and clinically as a Sexually Transmitted Disease — STD for short (but not to be confused with British Telecom, of course). My own sanguine outlook is perhaps coloured by my service in the RAF in Germany immediately after the war when I was attached to the Vice Squad in Hamburg, and that was an eye-opener, I assure you. One of my jobs was to interview airmen who 'caught it' and track down the infected partner and take her to hospital for treatment.

In the old days you weren't a man until you had had a dose of the clap. Shakespeare's plays are full of it. Henry VIII was reputedly syphilitic. Our present Queen's great-grandfather, King Edward VII, had gonorrhea and gave it to Queen Alexandra, according to A. Dickson Wright, a well-known Harley Street surgeon (whom older readers will recall as one of the finest after-dinner speakers of the day). He is quoted at length in a fascinating study of the subject by Theodor Rosebury (*Microbes and Morals*, Secker and Warburg 1971). Winston Churchill's father, Lord Randolph Churchill, died of syphilis, although most biographers just refer discreetly to his 'tragic death' without going into details. In fact, a roll-call of celebrities throughout history who had gonorrhea or syphilis would

more than fill the Distinguished Strangers' Gallery in the House of Commons — it would probably fill the Chamber itself.

Syphilis is a bit of an orphan. For years we called it the French disease. The French called it the Italian disease, the Portuguese the Spanish disease, the Japanese the Portuguese disease, the Polish the German disease, and the Russians the Polish disease. A sort of poxy pass-the-parcel. To put your mind at rest, the *English* disease was, and still is, for the Germans at least — rickets.

For all that, VD has what you might call an illustrious pedigree. One of the Pharaohs, Rameses V, had it 3,000 years ago and Julius Caesar and Cleopatra were also sufferers (sorry to shatter your illusions). And Christopher Columbus, Napoleon, and Nelson.

It is well represented in the arts. Beethoven's deafness was attributed to syphilis, Schubert certainly had it, Donizetti died of cerebral syphilis, and Schumann and Delius exhibited symptoms. In the world of painting Goya, Gauguin, Van Gogh, Manet, Toulouse-Lautrec, and our own Sir William Orpen are pre-eminent in the list of the love-scarred. In literature the names are legion. We all know about Boswell, but what of Keats and Thackeray and Oscar Wilde (admittedly better known for another sexual phenomenon), Schopenhauer (the entrenched misogynist, and no wonder), Nietzsche, Alfred de Musset, Flaubert, Baudelaire and Dostoevsky — all 'bitten by a Winchester goose' (so called after the Bishop of Winchester who was in charge of brothels in the fourteenth century)?

And we mustn't miss Lord Cardigan who gave his name to the woollies you see in Marks and Sparks today. He is also remembered for leading the disastrous charge of the Light Brigade at Balaclava in 1854, 'possibly unhinged', to quote Theodor Rosebury, 'by reason of a severely painful gonorrhea'. This is not mentioned, of course, in the famous poem by Lord Tennyson. Probably difficult to rhyme, I should think.

You wouldn't think syphilis a likely subject for a play, and certainly not in Victorian times. But it formed the basis of a classic tragedy still in the modern repertoire — Ibsen's *Ghosts,* and very daring it was too when it was first produced a century ago. In fact, although Ibsen was a Norwegian the play horrified his countrymen and its première had to be moved to Chicago. Make of that what you will. Finally, as regards gonorrhea, otherwise known as 'the clap', did you know that when you say somebody is 'clapped out' you are saying in effect he or she is debilitated by gonorrhea? If you don't believe me, look it up in the *OED.*

STDs are currently very widespread. New cases seen in NHS clinics in 1983 in England alone came to over half a million, with men suffering more than women (309,040 against 238,397). Syphilis seems to have been knocked on the head (3,327 cases). The clap is still thriving (48,393) and herpes, a relatively new arrival on the scene, is quite a strong runner (16,534). Herpes, being almost incurable, has given our swinging society something to think about. A current sardonic riddle asks what is the difference between love and herpes? Answer: herpes is for ever. But both of these are quite outstripped by candidiasis (57,876), a type of thrush predominantly afflicting women and by far the most prevalent single STD for women.

The law is surprisingly liberal towards STDs and there are no penalties for giving it to somebody, not disclosing it, or not submitting to treatment. However, no person other than a duly qualified medical practitioner may *for reward* (my italics) treat any person for VD or give any advice in connection with proposed treatment. This is laid down in the Venereal Disease Act 1917 but since the definition of VD in the Act is limited to 'syphilis, gonorrhea or soft chancre' there seems to be a slight loophole for STDs not known in 1917. If you give *free* advice you will be clear.

It is also a criminal offence to advertise that you can treat VD (again as defined by the Act) whether or not you are a doctor, although now that solicitors, accountants, and architects can display their wares in the market place it may not be long before doctors will be putting little semi-display ads in your local paper.

However, in *civil* law it seems that you can sue for damages if someone gives you an STD and serious harm results, and if you get it from your spouse it could be grounds for divorce.

I have not mentioned AIDS (Acquired Immune Deficiency Syndrome) which has recently frightened the life out of our transatlantic cousins with the death of Rock Hudson and thousands of others. Actresses in *Dallas* and *Dynasty* (now, I believe, pronounced 'die nasty') have gone on record that they won't kiss their co-stars unless they undergo a blood test beforehand. AIDS is not strictly an STD but state surveillance all over the world now seems to be the name of the game.

Curiously, it is not an offence to read library books if you've got a dose, as it *is* if you've got any of the notifiable diseases (there are 29 of them listed at the moment) such as hepatitis or green monkey fever, etc. If you have any of these and don't tell the library immediately you can be fined under Section 25 of the Public Health (Control of Disease) Act 1984.

But STDs, although of course communicable, are not 'notifiable'. Dr Bahl, who is in charge of community medicine in my neck of the woods in North London, tells me this is because it is current DHSS thinking that if they were, it would discourage those infected from seeking treatment.

ABORTION

There are about 120 million live births in the world every year. At least 12 million but perhaps as many as 30 million conceptions are estimated to end annually as induced abortions (UN Conference on World Population) — that is, more than 80,000 each day. In 1984 just under 170,000 abortions were carried out in England and Wales, that is just under 500 a day. This represented 20 per cent of all pregnancies since live births came to 678,000. Figures have shot up from 1969 (54,000 abortions) but since 1980 they have remained pretty constant at 160,000 plus. Of these the number of foreign visitors for this purpose has also remained fairly static at around 33,000.

Abortion is still illegal in Eire and Northern Ireland so it was no surprise to see that 5,476 colleens contributed to that figure. The highest invisible earnings though came from Spain. In 1969 just 11 Spanish women came to London for abortions. By 1985 the figure had shot up to 20,060. The vast majority of foreigners (99.7 per cent) have their abortions done privately. I culled these figures from an expensive government report produced annually called *Abortion Statistics*. It is 70 pages long, A4 size and covers the subject in a lot of detail.

How many girls of 15 and under do you think had abortions in 1984? I shall tell you: 5,609. And between 16 and 19 years old? 38,492. If you have a daughter, as I have, I think you'll find these figures a bit chilling. The Court of Appeal in the Gillick case ruled (reversing the decision of the trial judge) that an abortion on a girl under 16 may only be performed with the consent of her parent(s), except in a case of emergency, but this position was overruled in the House of Lords in 1985 — as long as the doctor exercises his bona fide professional judgement he is OK.

One or two other nuggets:
— Most abortions take place in the first quarter of the year (1 January to 31 March) possibly as a result of Christmas carelessness.
— Of the 136,000 abortions on resident women here (i.e. excluding the 33,000 foreigners) 76,500 were done privately (56 per cent).
— The most vulnerable age group is 20-24 (50,000).
— Very few women die following an abortion. The average over the last five years has been three a year.
— The overwhelming grounds for abortion are 'risk of injury to physical or mental health' (150,000 out of a total of 170,000).

It goes without saying that faulty methods of contraception or the complete lack of any precautions are the main causes of unwanted pregnancies. Young unmarried women are not alone in taking chances. Of all fertile married women not intending to get pregnant, 1 in 7 takes a chance at least sometimes, 1 in 14 regularly.

More than a third of abortions are performed on married women.

As for other countries, in Japan, which has been called 'a condom society', ('Abortion' CIBA Foundation Symposium 115, 1985) since both oral contraception (the Pill) and IUDs are illegal, the estimated percentage of pregnancies which end in abortion is 46 per cent (against 20 per cent in England and Wales). In 1981 in the USA about 1.5 million recorded legal abortions were performed, that is 25 per cent of all pregnancies, although it seems the actual figure is much higher, boosted by unreported operations.

With the passing of the Abortion Act in 1967 the days of the seedy back street abortionist were numbered. There was no need any more to drink a bottle of gin in a boiling hot bath (an old wives' dubious recipe) to get rid of an unwanted child. The Act (which does not apply to Northern Ireland, as I have said) is short and sharp and to the point. It consists of just six pithy clauses but these were enough to open the flood gates. The Act is also a model of clarity and worth quoting. An abortion may be carried out — but only by a registered medical practitioner (let's say a doctor), if *two* doctors believe:

> that the continuance of the pregnancy would involve risk to the life of the pregnant woman, or of injury to the physical or mental health of the pregnant woman or any existing children of her family, greater than if the pregnancy were terminated or by that there is a substantial risk that if the child were born it would suffer from such physical or mental abnormalities as to be seriously handicapped.

To decide whether the woman's health would be affected 'account may be taken of the pregnant woman's actual or reasonably foreseeable environment'. So you see the law bends over backwards to accommodate you. You can virtually have abortion on demand.

However a doctor or nurse is at liberty to refuse to take part in an abortion if on religious or other grounds they have a conscientious objection to doing so. Needless to say there are enormous variations of 'conscience'. Steer clear of the Birmingham area. The figures speak for themselves. Of 913 abortions in Dudley only 15, i.e. 1 in 60 were done on the NHS, while in Norwich and West Glamorgan the ratio was 54 in 60. This can only mean that gynaecologists are dead against abortion in Birmingham and won't let you have it on the NHS but all for it in certain other parts of the country. Worth a train ticket to get the law interpreted in your favour.

This apart, the doctors who see you have a very wide discretion to terminate a pregnancy. In fact only one doctor's opinion is needed if the abortion is immediately necessary in an emergency. Usually the abortion must be carried out in an NHS hospital or an approved private clinic. Very often a doctor may want to discuss your intentions with your husband, or partner, if you are unmarried. *He cannot do so without your consent* although in practice it may be very difficult to find two doctors who are willing to act without first consulting your husband. But the law is quite clear that the husband cannot stop the abortion. In the case of Paton v. BPAS (1978) a woman had not consulted her husband, who sought an injunction forbidding her to go ahead. He got nowhere. On the other hand, it is possible a husband could use his wife's insistence on an abortion as evidence of unreasonable behaviour for a divorce petition. Timing is very important. The law says that an abortion can only be performed in the first 28 weeks of pregnancy. Private nursing homes have guidelines not to do anything after 24 weeks and most NHS hospitals keep this down to 16 weeks. Your own doctor may be reluctant to consent to it after even 12 weeks. Most countries outside England and Wales — including the USSR where state abortions began — draw the line at 12 weeks. I understand that when you want a baby the nine months pass very slowly: when you don't they go by in a flash. So you must act quickly. If you go to your GP he will usually refer you to a consultant gynaecologist and all this takes time. Of course, many women quite genuinely get

mixed up with the dates of their periods and others consciously take off a month or two when they give these details to their doctor. To be on the safe side, ask your doctor to telephone the consultant for an appointment rather than write. If you find your doctor is unhelpful (he doesn't have to be your family doctor) you have another two options.
1. You can go to a family planning clinic or one of the non-profit-making agencies such as the BPAS (they defended the wife in the Paton case referred to above) or the PAS, who will give you good advice.
2. You can go direct to an approved private clinic (you will find details of these in Yellow Pages under 'Clinics', 'Family Planning' or 'Pregnancy Testing Services'). They are strictly regulated but openly commercial concerns and provided you meet the requirements of the Act you are rarely turned away, although they will never knowingly operate on anybody under the age of 16 without permission from the authorities. The going rate is about £145 which I gather compares favourably with clinics to which you are likely to be referred by the advisory services I have mentioned.

Never approach somebody to do the job who is not a doctor. The law is very strict about this. You mustn't try and abort the baby yourself or as the law puts it 'procure (your) own miscarriage' or get somebody to do it for you. The maximum penalty is imprisonment for *life* as provided in the Offences against the Person Act 1861, sections 58 and 59, which are still in force.

Older readers may recall the case of a very courageous and well-known Harley Street surgeon, a Mr Bourne, which made headlines in 1938. He is commemorated by a maternity ward named after him (the Aleck Bourne Ward) at St Mary's Hospital, Paddington where the Princess of Wales has her children. He terminated the pregnancy of a girl of 14 who had been raped by two Guardsmen. This was in the days when both the law and society took a very dim view of abortion. Mr Bourne was charged at the Old Bailey under section 58 of the Act but got off by the skin of his teeth after the Judge liberally interpreted the Act in his favour.

ot here is legally required to
register the birth within 42 days. The father of our own
Queen Mother was fined, according to Penelope Mortimer
(*Queen Elizabeth, Life of the Queen Mother*, Viking 1986),
for failing to report her birth on time and then risked 'penal
servitude for life by falsifying her place of birth'.

Finally, some myths surrounding abortion according to
Dr Michael Carrera (*Sex: The Facts, The Acts and Your
Feelings*, Mitchell Beazley 1981). There are no truths in
any of these statements:
— abortion is illegal in most countries
— only poor people have abortions
— you can't have a normal pregnancy once you've had a
  termination
— all religious groups oppose abortion
— if a woman has one abortion she will probably have
  several more
— pregnancy termination is medically a very risky
  business
— women who have abortions usually have long-term
  psychological problems
— most adults believe that abortion should be made illegal
— abortion is a modern issue, and results from a recent
  decline in moral standards
So, if you must, go ahead with a clear conscience.

BUMS

Can you get into trouble for making an adverse reference
to someone's behind? You certainly can if you are a
television critic like Miss Nina Myskow. She made some
very rude comments in the *News of the World* about the
singing ability and appearance of the actress Charlotte
Cornwell, including the size of her behind. Apparently

52

Miss Cornwell is well endowed in the nether parts and although many may think it a gift of the gods, Miss Cornwell does not. The Judge spent some time in getting to the bottom of the argument. His reasoning, as law students will understand, was *a posteriori*, of course, and he told the jury in December 1985 it was for them to decide the fundamental issue of whether Miss Myskow's review 'went beyond the bounds of acceptable TV criticism'. They thought it did and awarded Miss Cornwell £10,000 in libel damages.

I don't know why we usually regard bums as a big joke — a joke which cuts across all national frontiers. There is the story of the English born-again politician who had suddenly seen the light in middle-age — a sort of latterday Malcolm Muggeridge — who went to France on a lecture tour explaining his conversion. He would start his speech by saying that when he looked back on his past he saw that it was divided in two parts, before and after he saw the light. Only his French wasn't up to it, and he would say *'Quand je regarde mon derrière, je trouve qu'il est divisé en deux parties'* (when I look at my behind I find that it is divided in two parts).

3

HOUSE AND GARDEN

ESTATE AGENTS

If you give an estate agent a 'sole agency' this means that
you will not use any other estate agent. The sole agent can
stop you from using another agent and take you to court.
Or, if you do use another agent, you may end up paying
two lots of commission. Beware of giving an agent 'sole
selling rights'. If you do, and then sell your house privately
(say to a friend) you still have to pay his commission. Limit
the arrangement to a specific period and you will be home
and dry. If you want to sell your house quickly you may
decide to put your property with several different estate
agents in your area. But be careful. If you sell it to someone
who has been around and got your name from three or four
agents they could all send you a bill. Know from the start
which agent sent you which prospective purchaser.

Life isn't very straightforward, is it?

BUYING AND SELLING

Surely if you are selling your house you can sell it to
whomever you wish, assuming the offered price is right.
This is not true. If you advertise to sell your house or put
it with an agent you can't refuse to sell on grounds of
colour, race or nationality. So be careful before you show
any potential buyer the door; not only will he go up the
wall and probably hit the roof but you will be dropping
a large brick.

When you walk into an estate agency you are often given
a fact-sheet describing the place you want. Usually in very
small print at the bottom there is a disclaimer (i.e. a
repudiation) of any liability by the agent or vendor for
incorrectly describing the property. You buy the house or
whatever and find you were misled, for example it was a

house not yet built and the fact-sheet said a lawn would
be laid but this was not put in the actual contract you
signed when you exchanged contracts. You can still make
the vendor lay the lawn or give you the money to do it.
He cannot hide behind the disclaimer. The test is one of
'reasonableness'.

Don't believe everything you read or hear (my
grandfather used to say only believe half of what you read
and nothing of what you hear). This also applies to
surveyors. You get a survey report. It says there was no
woodworm or dry rot or wet rot as far as the surveyor could
tell but he could not take up the carpets so his inspection
was limited. You buy the place and find it riddled with
woodworm and dry rot. What is the second thing you do?
You sue the surveyor for negligence because his disclaimer
is a lot of rot, dry wet or tommy — take your pick (the *first*
thing you do is see your solicitor, of course).

BEWARE OF LEASEHOLDS
Have you ever owned a leasehold flat, office or shop? You
have? And were you the first person to buy the lease? Then
here's something that can give you insomnia. Let's assume
that you took on a new lease for 99 years. After a few years
you sold the lease, moved on. Since then the lease has
changed hands several times. You have lost track. It has
nothing to do with you. Or has it? According to the law,
if the present tenant goes bust or does a moonlight flit
leaving behind arrears of rent the original landlord could
sue you for all the money. And this goes for service charges
too — in fact, all debts due to the landlord.

Yes, you. Because you are the original tenant and are
liable for the entire period of the lease. What's more, if the
premises cannot be let you have to carry on paying the rent,
no matter how high it goes — and the service charges —
until the full 99 years are up. More bad news — if you
cannot pay, you can be made bankrupt. Surprised? The
law *is* surprising. In my view this is totally wrong and a
shrewd MP would have all our support if he brought in
a Bill to change the law. After all, general rates and water

rates are legally payable solely by the *occupier* of the premises. If they are not paid, earlier or later occupiers cannot be pursued for them. Why should it be otherwise for rent and service charges?

SERVICE CHARGES ON LONG LEASES OF PRIVATE FLATS

This is becoming a very fraught area. More and more landlords are being exposed in the media for their shortcomings if not downright rapacity. Mr Michael Montague, Chairman of the National Consumer Council, is spearheading a drive against abuses of the system, but sadly he doesn't seem to be getting very far. One very insidious development has recently come to the fore equalling the Rachmanism of the 1960s. This is when a born-again Victorian grasping landlord sends in grossly inflated or even completely fictitious charges for maintenance backed up by solicitors 'pay up or else' threats. Or he may get money as a result of a genuine claim against an insurance company (say for structural defects of the building and so on) and put it in his pocket. He then sells the block of flats. The new owner knows nothing and the tenant has to pick up the pieces.

The law is a maze for most laymen and if you are getting on in years sometimes quite incomprehensible. Imagine you are a widow in your sixties or seventies subjected to this type of harrassment. It can worry the life out of you. What can you do about it? Well, first of all, your rights and obligations are all spelt out in your lease and go under the name of 'covenants', the lessor's covenants defining what the landlord has to do, the lessee's covenants what you have to do. Secondly, these should be read in conjunction with the Housing Act 1980 which gives you very important protection. A word of warning. Don't try and read it yourself. If you don't suffer from acute depression already I assure you that you will after trying to make head or tail of this brainchild of our legal draftsmen. The best thing is to mosey off to your local Citizens Advice Bureau or library and get a free leaflet called *Service Charges in Flats* which is very readable and explains the workings of the Act, at least in theory. You will see in it that the word 'reasonable' keeps cropping up. The standard of services must be 'reasonable', the cost of the services must be 'reasonable', if you are asked to pay some money in advance the amount demanded must be 'reasonable' and so on. Now I know this is not much consolation because if you refuse to pay charges on the grounds that they are unreasonable your landlord could take you to court, and if he is neglecting his contractual duty as a landlord you will have to take him to court. But as I tell my clients time and time again, your legal rights are one thing — *enforcing* them is another. It has been rightly said that the Courts of England are open to all her citizens — like the doors of the Ritz Hotel.

But take heart. If all the tenants band together you will find unity is strength. If you don't want to be militant and think you may upset your landlord — think again. *This is your home,* not to say your castle. Worry your MP. See a solicitor: you may possibly get legal aid, and the law will be on your side. Here is one tip worth knowing. If your landlord is not getting on with essential repairs and maintenance you may well get your local council to serve an improvement notice and if necessary prosecute under an astute interpretation of the Health and Safety at Work Act 1974. Westminster City Council did exactly this with Select Management Ltd and the Court of Appeal agreed with them. Good on you, Westminster! It's all in *The Times Law Report* of 19 February 1985, which you can read at the library.

Further, in my view sending fictitious bills to old ladies — or even young ones — followed by threats, is a form of harassment, and could possibly even be construed as demanding money with menaces (blackmail), clearly a criminal offence. Under the Administration of Justice Act 1970 Section 40:

a person commits an offence, if with the object of coercing another person to pay money claimed from that other as a debt due under a contract he 1.) harasses that other with demands for payments which because of their frequency or their manner or occasion of making any such demands, or of any threat or publicity by which any demand is accompanied, are calculated to subject him or members of his family or household to alarm, distress or humiliation ...

This seems to fit the bill. The maximum fine is £2,000 and an order can be made for the landlord to pay compensation for mental upset you suffer. You may also have a remedy under the Rent Act 1965 Section 30 which was designed to stamp out Rachmanism. But see page 59.

A much more severe penalty (imprisonment for up to seven years) is imposed by the Theft Act 1968 for what is called 'false accounting'. If Lord Denning were still a Judge he might well tap this source of law to make rogue landlords put their house or houses in order.

If you are a flat dweller, you can see that the law needs more teeth — in fact the whole leasehold concept is in dire need of overhaul. Could it be scrapped altogether and replaced by strata freeholds as in Australia? Why not? When you are asked what you want for Christmas just ask for a British Ralph Nader who turned US industry and society on its head. If we had Ralph Nader here perhaps he might bring more pressure to bear on the banks and buildings societies to whom landlords (good and bad) very often turn to finance their property dealings. We hear a lot about great British institutions investing in South Africa and I am sure there are arguments for and against. What about our banks checking the uses to which their money is put in our own country? Some comeuppance called for?

One more point about flats. Say you live in a block of them and leave your keys with the porter. One day while you are away the porter lets himself into your flat — without your permission — and makes off with your jewellery. You are not insured. Even if you are there was obviously no forced entry and the insurance company might wriggle out of meeting a claim. (Insurance companies are often quite good at this.) The porter has disappeared. Can you get any compensation from the landlords or managing agents? Yes, you can, in certain circumstances. The High Court has recently held in such a case that the landlords and agents were liable and had to pay up because the porter had 'form'. He had a criminal record and more care should have been taken when he was given the job. As Lord Arran once remarked, 'it's not the people who are in prison who worry me. It's the people who aren't.'

NO LONGER A LICENCE TO PRINT MONEY

The Rent Acts were brought in some years ago to give protection to tenants of rented property. If you are a protected tenant your landlord is prevented from giving you notice to quit except in certain restricted cases. You have what is called 'security of tenure' and what is more, you can ask for a fair rent to be fixed.

But to get round the law some landlords have resorted to all sorts of devices. They put a box of Kelloggs and a pot of tea and a couple of boiled eggs outside your door in the mornings and get somebody to make your bed. This brings them outside the Acts since they are providing 'services'. They can charge you as much as they like and kick you out if you make a fuss. Or they give you a 'holiday let' for six months with the same results. Though whether six months in the winter in Bermondsey can be considered a holiday is, I think, debatable. A ruse much in favour is to give you a 'licence' instead of a rental agreement, since a genuine licence also escapes the rigours of the Acts.

But there is good news for tenants put upon by these shams. In April 1985 a Mrs Wendy Mountford went to the House of Lords to appeal against a Court of Appeal ruling that she had only a licence and not a tenancy of two furnished rooms she occupied exclusively in a house near Bournemouth for which she paid £37 per week. The five law lords came down on her side unanimously, even though the agreement she had signed when she took the rooms from her landlord, a Mr Street (a solicitor, no less), expressly stated that she accepted that her licence to occupy the flat did not give her a tenancy protected by the Rent Acts. When she applied for a fair rent to be registered the landlord asked her to leave and you would have thought that it was an open and shut case. Their lordships, however, ruled in favour of Mrs Mountford, even though she had signed away her protection under the Rent Acts. In the words of Lord Templeman, 'It was plain that Mrs Mountford was not a lodger. Where ... residential accommodation is offered and accepted with exclusive possession [i.e. nobody else uses your room or rooms] for a term at a rent the result is a tenancy.' He went on to say 'the manufacture of a five-pronged implement for manual digging results in a fork even if the manufacturer... insisted that he intended to make... a spade'. I believe this is what is known as calling a fork a fork, or perhaps a spade a spade. Their lordships certainly dug it.

To adapt a popular saying — you can fool some of our Judges all of the time and all our Judges some of the time but you can't fool all our Judges all the time.

Who said we should abolish the House of Lords?

DOORS AND WINDOWS OPENING ONTO THE PAVEMENT

If you have a house or shop did you know that the doors or garden gates must not open outwards, only inwards — unless you get permission from the appropriate authority, which is rarely given. The Highways Act 1980 specifically prohibits this. Say your *windows* at ground floor level open on to the pavement. The Highways Act only refers to 'doors' etc. So you think you have spotted a loophole. Forget it. You could be caught under the Town Police Clauses Act 1847 which makes it an offence to obstruct the public footpath. And this also goes for blinds and awnings. All parts of the blind or awning must be at least 8 feet in height from every part of the ground. The funny thing is that I have seen loads of shop blinds which I can reach quite easily with my hand, and I assure you I am not 7 feet tall.

RATES, TENANCIES AND FIRE

RATES AND YOUR NEIGHBOURS
Can you get your rates reduced if your neighbours make a nuisance of themselves and so affect the enjoyment of your home? Surprisingly, yes. St Valentine's Day — 14 February — 1986 was not a case of love your neighbour for Mrs Pat McSorley in Windsor, Berkshire when she applied to a rating valuation panel to reduce the rateable value of her home. The court was sympathetic to Mrs McSorley's claim that her life had become like something from a horror movie after a group of Hell's Angels had moved in next door. She told the court how they had exposed themselves to her, thrown axes around the back garden, cavorted with samurai swords and urinated and vomited in public. Her appeal for a rate reduction was challenged by Windsor and Maidenhead council who claimed that neighbours were not a reason to reduce the rateable value. However, the Court found in Mrs McSorley's favour and cut the rateable value from £337 to a nominal £1.

Don't think it's all that simple to get your rating valuation revised. In March 1986 two spinster sisters living in Barnes, Dr Sheila Tangye and Hilary Tangye, complained that the man next door was holding nude swimming parties in his indoor pool, and his revels disturbed them. No luck. They just had to go on being affronted.

Which brings to mind the rather old story of the lady who rang up the police one evening to say that a man across the way was indecently exposing himself by walking around his flat in the altogether. When the police arrived and looked, they said they could see nothing. 'Of course you can't', said the lady. 'You've got to switch off the light and stand on a chair to see it properly.'

TENANCIES
There are a number of terms used to describe residential tenancies. Among these are 'protected' tenancies,

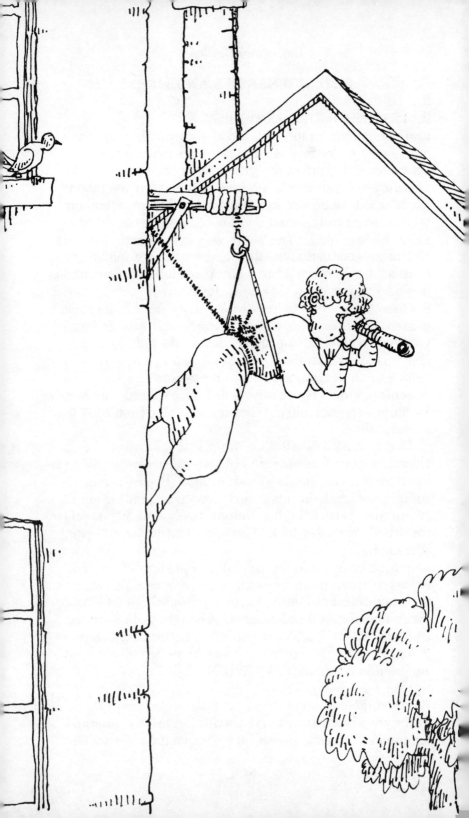

'statutory' tenancies and 'regulated' tenancies. ('Controlled' tenancies went out in 1981 when they all became 'regulated'.) A tenancy is protected while the lease originally granted by the landlord exists. (A protected tenancy is often referred to as a 'contractual' tenancy because it only goes on as long as the contract of tenancy is in existence.) At the end of a protected tenancy a 'statutory' tenancy arises in favour of the person who is then resident in the house or flat. This statutory tenancy continues until you leave the property, for whatever reason. All these tenancies are called 'regulated'.

By the way, there is very little distinction nowadays between unfurnished tenancies and furnished tenancies. Subject to rateable values and one or two other conditions nearly all tenants enjoy the protection of the Rent Acts.

Now if you live in a council house or wherever and you go bankrupt or die, what happens? If you are a *protected* tenant your tenancy is said to vest in the trustee in bankruptcy and if the trustee disclaims the tenancy you have no further right to possession. This means simply that the person who is appointed to supervise your affairs when you become bankrupt can decide whether you can stay or go. But if you are a *statutory* tenant and become bankrupt your tenancy just carries on. When you die as a statutory tenant your tenancy passes automatically to your husband or wife. If you are not married the tenancy can pass to any member of the family who lived with you during the last six months of your life. This transfer of the tenancy is called a 'transmission' and while 'member of the family' has not been defined, it includes close relatives and possibly also a mistress, at least if there are children. A transmission can take place twice. Say you die and your wife takes over and then she dies, your son can take over, provided in each case the party concerned lived with you for the previous six months. Once the *second* party dies the landlord can recover possession. No further transmissions are allowed. Here's an interesting point. If a member of the family takes over when you die and for various reasons you had accumulated huge arrears of rent, does your successor have to pay them, if he or she wants to stay in the home? No, they don't. This was a judicial decision as long ago as 1929 (Tickner v. Clifton).

Do you know what the rent arrears owed by council tenants in 1985 came to? The figures were given in Parliament recently (*Hansard*, 19 February 1986). In inner London alone they came to £57 million. Top of the pops was Southwark (£10,965,216), with Hackney a close contender (£9,228.000, a figure which represented 27 per cent of the rent roll). And that doesn't include arrears of rates.

ORDEAL BY FIRE
Do you have to go on paying rent if your rented home, house or flat, is destroyed by fire or flooding etc? There is no clear-cut answer. In fact, there have been cases when the tenant had to pay the rent after the premises were totally destroyed (Matthey v. Curling, 1922) and even one in which the landlord had been compensated by his insurance company and refused to rebuild (Lofft v. Dennis, 1859). Received legal wisdom nowadays is that where the whole purpose of the tenancy is frustrated, it comes to an end. But this has not yet been conclusively decided and a test case is awaited.

It's still a very grey area, if not a burning issue.

TREES, BATS, COCKROACHES AND WILD PLANTS

SOME FRUITFUL ADVICE
Do you have a garden? Someone could be leading you up the garden path. Your neighbour. His tree overhangs your garden but he refuses to trim the branches. Do you stay in the shade? The law says you can cut off his branches at the boundary line. But you must return the branches and any fruit.

What about fruit which falls into your garden? This belongs to your neighbour and cannot be used without his consent. But you have no legal obligation to hand it back or even allow it to be collected. What is more he can take no legal action against you for its return.

Quite an interesting branch of the law. Be careful — do it right, or you may find yourself out on a limb.

BATS IN THE BELFRY
Yes, the Nature Conservancy Council are at it again. They circulated a reminder in 1985 to people with bats in their property that all species of British bat are protected by law. Since there's as yet no official Bat Registration Council I wouldn't know how they contact you but that's their business. This followed a prosecution of a Yorkshire firm who were fined £1,000 plus £350 costs for disturbing a colony of bats in the loft of a house being treated for woodworm. The charge was brought under the Wildlife and Countryside Act 1981 as amended.

What would you rather have, bats or woodworm? Shiver my timbers, I wouldn't want either, and if I can't get rid of a smelly flock of bats under my own roof without Big Brother tapping me on the shoulder I can only conclude the world is not yet safe for democracy.

Reading of this prosecution prompted me to look up the Act. I found that bats are only one of several species protected. Among the others — and they're all called 'Protected Wild Animals' — are rainbow leaf beetles, wart-biter grasshoppers, black-veined moths, glutinous snails, smooth snakes, and fen raft spiders, without any of which, of course, no self-respecting ratepayer would consider his household worthy of the name. Would you believe it is a criminal offence 'intentionally to disturb any such animal so listed while it is occupying a structure or place which it uses for shelter or protection'? Or 'to damage or destroy or *obstruct access* to such a structure or place'? Or attempt any of these wanton acts? It is. I think you can still swat flies, and there seems to be no objection to putting up a No Entry sign in your garden to stop snakes playing with the baby. But watch yourself with spiders: they have legal rights too. You have been warned.

COCKROACHES
I think it is a bit of a status symbol to have cockroaches

nowadays since both the Café Royal and Brooks Club have been fined for cockroach infestation. In 1983 Trust House Forte had to cough up £675 for not keeping the Café kitchens bug-free.

There was a recent case heard in the county court involving cockroaches on a council estate when damages of over £1,000 for discomfort were awarded in 1985 to a tenant who complained that his landlords, the local authority, hadn't dealt with them properly (Hudson v. Royal Borough of Kensington and Chelsea). This was a very important case and seems to have opened the floodgates for tenants to claim against landlords for vermin of this kind. So if you find cockroaches in your flat and can't get rid of them because they are crawling all over the block just write a polite letter to your landlord pointing out the ruling in this case and he should fall over himself to put matters right. At least that's the theory.

WILD PLANTS
> *Mary, Mary, quite contrary,*
> *How does your garden grow?*

Believe it or not, the batty nonsense just mentioned applies, *mutatis mutandis*, as the lawyers say (this just means 'in the same way'), to wild plants in your own backyard. I am a self-confessed townie. I don't want to hurt your feelings, and if you hold strong botanical views I will defer to them. But you should know it is again a criminal offence intentionally to pick or uproot — or attempt to — any one of a list of plants as long as a rake. I admit the list reads for the most part quite lyrically, from Snowdon lilies to fen violet and brown galingale — although I don't know what to make of drooping saxifrage and Dickie's bladder fern. No doubt seasoned gardeners will put me on the right path.

A difficulty now arises. How can you tell a Dickie's bladder etc from a naked lady, which is a poisonous weed? No problem at all for the Nature Conservancy Council. The NCC, bless 'em, know all the answers. What they suggest you do if in doubt is:

1. leave the plant alone
2. photograph it
3. contact either one of their regional offices or the Botanical Society of the British Isles for verification. The address of the Society is Oundle Lodge, Oundle, Peterborough PE8 5TN.

Now, before you get your car out of the garage, take a grip on yourself and consider your best move. You have several options. The chief two are:

1. to plan your submissions carefully to put before the Society
2. to watch Match of the Day and let your garden run wild. I know what I would do. It's a fair distance from Hampstead to Peterborough and I'm not much of a gardener.

Two last things you should know. One, it is also an offence to possess 'any thing capable of being used' to commit the offences I have described. So for goodness sake hide those garden shears in a safe place beyond the reach of the NCC inspectors, else you're for it. And two, don't start growing Japanese seaweed in the garden, or giant hogweed or kelp. I can't help feeling this was in your mind but according to the Act it's just as heinous an offence as picking drooping saxifrage.

Happy gardening, nonetheless.

4

ANIMALS

PETS

Dogs aren't enough any more, Men need elephants.
                                        Romain Gary

Byron, the great Romantic poet, used to keep a bear in his rooms when he was up at Cambridge. He didn't think much of the college dons and wanted the bear to sit for a fellowship. Gérard de Nerval, a French poet, used to lead a lobster around the streets of Paris. But he suffered from hallucinations (the poet, that is, not the lobster) and presumably thought it was a retarded chihuahua.

Have *you* ever felt the urge to keep a different sort of pet in the back garden of your semi? You may feel that a man's best friend is his bactrian camel or hippopotamus. Or giraffe, gorilla, or crocodile. The good news is that you can, and show that attractive widow two doors up what sort of chap you really are. Well — why shouldn't you keep a dik-dik ('a small African antelope' according to the *OED*, but a dangerous wild animal according to the law) if you feel he needs a good home? And there's nothing like showing off your dik-dik to the neighbours. It could be quite trendy in fact. Although all these pets are regarded legally as 'dangerous wild animals', all you have to do is apply to your local council for a licence. Of course, you have to meet certain conditions but they are not very tiresome: you have to be over 18 years old, your pet must have room to exercise, he has got to behave and not be a nuisance, and so on.

If you can't be bothered to go through all this rigmarole but still want to make a personal statement, why not settle for a llama? No jokes please about Tibetan priests. You will

of course know that a llama is a sort of Peruvian camel
without a hump (your neighbour will be the one with the
hump) used as a beast of burden in the Andes. And you
never know, your wife may welcome another beast of
burden around the house. I say llama because this pet, in
common with domestic cats and dogs, pigs and aardwolves
(a species of hyena, no less), is not considered to be a
dangerous wild animal and doesn't need a licence.

Happy hunting.

VAMPIRE BATS

When animals which may be subject to rabies, such as cats
and dogs or elephants or giraffes, are brought into the
country, they have to go into quarantine for six months
under the Rabies Order 1974. However, there's one
exception, and that's when you bring in a vampire bat. I'm
sure the thought of having one must occur from time to
time to every — er — red-blooded male. Think twice before
you decide to keep a bat, even a straight bat, as we were
urged at school. If you can't resist the temptation, know

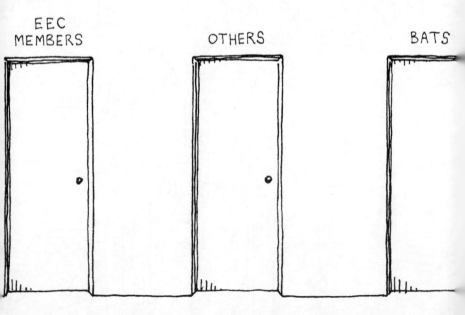

now it will not be a question of 'my place or yours?' It will always be his, or hers, as these poor creatures are given a life sentence as soon as they set claw on our shores. Under the Order they are quarantined for *life*. Not much fun for bats, who hang upside down most of the time anyway. And even more frustrating for members of the Transylvanian aristocracy, if their family name happens to be Dracula.

Why are these bats treated to such an indignity? The Curator of Mammals at the London Zoo — our very own batman — told me (and he should know) that it was because they can be undetected *carriers* of rabies, and give it to you and me. Not like cats and dogs, who show the symptoms within six months if they're infected. So there. You wouldn't think anybody could write a romantic opera called *The Bat*, but Johann Strauss did (well, an operetta) — *Die Fledermaus*, which is the German for bat.

The French call bats 'bald mice' (*chauve-souris*). I thought you'd like to know.

SQUIRRELS, GAME, AND SHOOTING BIRDS

SQUIRRELS
Those endearing little chaps, bright-eyed and bushy-tailed, that you photograph in your garden holding acorns in their paws, are vermin in the eyes of some of our civil servants (the Forestry Commissioners) who have powers to enter your garden to kill them or take them away if they think their trees are, *or are likely to be*, damaged. To add insult to injury, you have to pay for this invasion of your privacy. If you don't you can be sued for the cost of killing them as a civil debt. And if you prevent your squirrels being put down you can be fined for obstruction.

I always thought squirrels went after nuts. Now it seems it's the other way round.

GAME
If you buy and sell rabbits do you need an official licence? Yes, in fact you need not one but two. If you are a dealer in game, as several butchers are, you must have both an

excise licence and a game-dealers' licence, which is an approval of the applicant's suitability to handle game under the Game Act 1831. You get both from your local or county council.

Did you know that the word 'game' has never been properly defined by Parliament? In different Acts there are different definitions of the word. Hares, rabbits and deer are the only four-legged animals considered as game and are called 'ground game'. The rest are, of course, wild birds such as pheasants and the like. There is no close season for rabbits or hares but you mustn't shoot or trap them or certain game birds on a Sunday or Christmas Day. And in London you must never use poison to kill hares or rabbits.

SHOOTING BIRDS
Can you shoot sparrows and starlings in your garden? The short answer is, sadly, yes. Although the Wildlife and Countryside Act 1981 was intended to protect all wild birds, their nests and eggs, it contains a list of birds (Schedule 2 Pt II) which may be killed or taken at all times by 'authorized persons'. The definition of 'authorized persons' includes the owner or occupier of the land where the bird is, or any person authorized by him (Section 27). Among others on the list are gulls, jays, magpies — and doves, the symbols of peace from Noah to Picasso...

Spare a moment for William Blake, the great poet who wrote 'Jerusalem'. He also wrote:
> A skylark wounded in the wing,
> A cherubim does cease to sing.

FARMER STUNG BY BEES
You are a farmer and you spray your field with insecticide — a fairly normal practice — to keep your crops healthy. Some bees fly over belonging to a neighbouring bee-keeper, to forage for pollen, or whatever bees forage for. The bees, being bees, do not realize that the plants on which they alight are full of poison and don't make it back home. Do you have to compensate the bee-keeper? Surprisingly enough, you do, or so it was held in the High Court in 1984

in Lewes, Sussex, when a group of five Sussex bee-keepers sued a farmer for damages after 33 colonies of their honey bees were destroyed following a visit to a field the farmer had sprayed with insecticide. It was argued strenuously on behalf of the farmer that a man can do whatever he likes on his own land as long as he is not malicious to others in his actions and as long as he does not affect his neighbour or anyone living nearby. The bees it was claimed were trespassers. I have some sympathy for this view since if a bee alights on me I regard its visit as an uninvited invasion of my privacy.

But the learned Judge ruled otherwise and declared that the farmer had to exercise the common duty of care towards his neighbours — in this case the bees — and awarded substantial compensation to be paid to the bee-keepers. So do be careful when you spray your rose bushes.

PRAWNS, SNAILS, FROGS AND WORMS

STARTING WITH PRAWNS ...
We are very touchy about our pets, in fact all animals, especially if they're cuddly. In November 1985 animal lovers at Kidderminster brought pressure on a fish and game merchant, Mr Barry Onslow, to remove the following notice from his shop: 'Watership Down — you've read the book, you've seen the film — now eat the cast'.

Now I wouldn't say prawns were cuddly. I remember a play *The Amorous Prawn* and I suppose scampi have their love life. But I would call them more chewy than cuddly. Yet, as *The Times* reported in March 1974, Eleanor Donoghy, a fish worker, appeared at Duns Sheriff Court, Berwickshire accused of ill treating prawns, a charge brought under the Protection of Animals (Scotland) Act 1912. How did she ill-treat them? She put them on a hotplate where they danced about like Mexican beans. I suppose if you had put Eleanor on a hotplate it would have produced a similar spectacle. But no tut-tutting please. Lobsters, as we all know, grace your dining table by being thrown alive into scalding water which gives them their tasteful shade of pink. Salmon and trout don't have much fun either, being battered to death after being yanked out of the river by a mallet, jocularly known in fishing circles since early Victorian times as a 'priest', a bit of black humour suggesting the administering of the last rites, although I understand this is not standard equipment for a Catholic priest when he visits you on your deathbed. Incidentally, the new legislation concerning animal experimentation requires any person using a fish to kill it by removing its head and destroying its brains. Rather barbaric, I'm sure you'll agree.

And the forcefeeding of geese to produce *paté de foie gras*? I won't even mention the detestable form of animal-baiting going under the name of bull-fighting, after which bulls end up as roast beef.

Coming back to Duns, this was the birthplace in 1265 of John Duns Scotus, a reactionary theologian and complete nutter. His name has gone down in history since he gave the word 'dunce' to the language. And this, you will see, is not all that irrelevant.

I discussed the prawns' case at length with Eleanor's solicitor, Mr Robert Mackay, and a very canny counsel he is too. He told me he advanced the ingenious argument in court that the Act only protected 'animals'. A prawn isn't an animal, nor is it a bird or a fish or a reptile. It's a crustacean, and the Act doesn't mention crustaceans. The court called for expert evidence and finally agreed with Mr Mackay. So Eleanor was let off the hook, so to speak, to applause from the public gallery, since Berwick fishwives are not to be trifled with, and allowed to go back and have her way with her prawns while Mr Mackay retired to lunch on a well-earned snack of Arbroath smokies.

A bit hard on the prawns, if you ask me, but I suppose it leaves scope for some ambitious MPs to bring in a Private Members Bill to protect these defenceless delicacies. Next time you tuck into some fried scampi spare them a thought. The prawns, I mean. MPs can look after themselves.

... AND CONTINUING WITH SNAILS

As I have indicated, the empathy of the animal rights movement knows no bounds. In 1985 the Independent Broadcasting Authority received a complaint after an advertisement was screened on television showing a punk snail, that is a snail dressed in beads and other finery, plugging the fact that the BBC's radio ratings were behind those of the independent radio companies.

Now I am an animal lover and I love snails too (preferably hot and with lots of garlic). I suppose you could regard the ad as 'a cruel infringement of normal standards of compassion', as the complaint was worded, particularly if you were a snail, although I imagine you wouldn't have strong feelings on the subject if you were a *dead* snail, as this one turned out to have been (Saatchi and Saatchi *never* use live snails on the telly). Jenny Crick, the lady in charge of the snail complaints department at the IBA, was very reassuring. She told me she took appropriate action on the complaint immediately and scotched any rumours that it had ended up in the dead (snail) letter file (but see page 65 'Bats in the belfry').

You will be interested to learn that the snail cadaver is now on show at a West End restaurant called *L'Escargot*. Naturally.

FROGS' LEGS

I have never cared much for frogs' legs. And now there is a move all over the world to stop dishing them up to satisfy Gallic gourmet palates. Apparently the bulk of frogs' legs come from Asia. Between them, Bangladesh, India and Indonesia export 200 million frogs a year. Yes, that's 400 million legs. Conservationists don't like it. They have taken legal action to list Asian bullfrogs as an endangered species. As the *Observer* reported in 1985, West Germany is to the forefront in protecting these hapless creatures. In addition to government support, a campaign called 'let the frogs keep their legs' has followed in the wake of a successful protest against turtle soup. More than 250 restaurants have banned frogs' legs from their menus.

'No luv...he either gets a speaking role
with full billing or he just wont do it!

Animals

In Britain we have developed a taste for these delicacies, which are a bit like chicken, I am told. Consumption increased from 13 tons in 1977 to more than 109 tons in 1983. But in 1984 Safeway foodstores — the first chain store to stock them — stopped its sales, saying it was not wholly satisfied with the treatment of frogs during processing. Good on you, Safeway. I never did hold with these foreign barbarities. Though if taken to its (eco)logical conclusion I suppose we'd all end up eating spaghetti and tinned fruit. I've never seen a lamb or calf slaughtered and I don't want to.

WORM-EATEN
Which brings me to worms, lugworms to be exact. In August 1985 three anglers were fined for digging for lugworms on the Northumberland coast. And quite right too. There you are, a lugworm minding your own business on a remote part of the English coast, when you're suddenly dug up. There's no justice, I can hear you say. Ah, but there was. The fishermen were taken to court.

Wait a minute. The prosecution was brought by the Nature Conservancy Council who you might think were there as stout defenders of the legal rights of lugworms. Not a bit. Their prime concern, as NCC regional officer Mr Mike Hudson explained, 'was not for the lugworm but to protect the birds who fed on them. The activities of bait diggers have prevented wildfowl and waders from feeding in quite substantial numbers and it was felt we had no alternative but to take action.'

Strictly for the birds, as you may well say. As the rhyme has it:

> Big fleas
> Have little fleas
> On their backs to bite 'em
> And little fleas
> Have smaller fleas
> And so *ad infinitum*.

CRUELTY TO ANIMALS SANCTIONED BY LAW
The RSPCA are pretty unanimous in their condemnation of the law's ambivalence towards animals. Mr Fred Comber, a senior RSPCA inspector, agrees with me that the law needs changing. I am not just thinking of fox-hunting and hare-coursing.

SPRING TRAPS
The Pest Act 1954 puts very strict controls on the sale or use of spring traps (if caught in one the animal usually suffers a lingering and painful death). But it is not illegal to make and sell them as curios or to own one. The Act says you mustn't have one in your posssession for an 'unlawful purpose'. Impossible to prove.

CRUELTY TO CATS, ETC.
Under the Protection of Animals (Cruelty to Dogs) Act 1922 if you are convicted of ill-treating a dog you can be immediately disqualified on a first offence from keeping a dog. But the law is much more lenient regarding cruelty to other animals who would normally only be taken from you if you already have a conviction for cruelty, i.e. if it's a *second* offence. This seems to be rather unfair on the family moggy.

MERCY KILLINGS
If a police constable finds or is called to any animal coming within the description of a farm animal (horse, bull, sheep, goat, etc) in such a state due to injury or disease that it would be cruel to move it and he can't trace the owner, or the owner won't give his consent, he *must* put it down after getting the authority of a vet (the vet has no legal powers to do it himself). But not *cats or dogs* for which no provision is made in the Act (Section 11 Protection of Animals Act 1911). As the law stands they can just be left to die a slow and distressing death.

BRANDING-IRONS
You'll be familiar with these if you watch Westerns. They

are now illegal here under the Welfare of Livestock (Prohibited Operations) Regulations 1982. But you can still hot-brand horses as much as you like. It seems they were overlooked when the Order was drafted.

SCALE OF FINES FOR ILL-TREATING DOGS
Another embarrassing oversight of our law-makers. Under the Protection of Animals Act 1911 as amended by the Criminal Justice Act 1982 the maximum penalty for cruelty to animals is £1,000. But under the Animal Health Act 1981 you can be fined up to £2,000 for not having a dog licence or dog collar. So it's cheaper to beat your dog to death than to be without a dog licence. However I should say that the legislation for dog licences is currently under review.

BESTIALITY — A SHAGGY DOG STORY
In 1984 a case was heard under the Sexual Offences Act 1956 (R. v. Higson). The facts were these: Mrs H. had returned home unexpectedly and found Mr H. on the carpet attempting to have intercourse with the family pet, a Pyrenean mountain bitch. She reported this untoward activity of her husband to the police who charged him under the Act, and he got two years. On appeal the sentence of imprisonment was reduced to a probation order. The marriage had been under strain for some time, and the Judge was sympathetic and concluded 'it was Mr H. who needed help, not the dog'.

Now, while this shows admirable concern by the Bench for the needs of the defendant, I find the Judge's dismissal of the needs of man's best friend quite improper and lacking in imagination. A psychiatrist could have been called to advise (on the dog, of course, not the Judge). To be charitable, it may be that Mr H. thought he was indeed catering to the dog's needs, albeit in a form unbargained for by the family pet lying quietly in front of the fire watching Wogan. I dare say it was affection of a kind.

5

ON THE ROAD

BREATHTAKING

I think it is true to say that most policemen are not Jewish. But did you know that if you are unlucky enough to be breathalysed, the officer who goes through the ritual of making you blow in the bag must keep his head covered? The Road Traffic Act 1972 states quite categorically that he must be 'a constable in uniform'. So he must have his hat or helmet on when he asks you for a sample of your breath. Think back. Did he have his hat on when he said 'Good evening, sir'? If he didn't you can breathe again.

Or were you too sloshed to notice?

Recently an important ruling was given in the House of Lords (Fox v. Gwent C.C. 1985). In this case a driver had been followed home by the police who suspected him of being drunk. They knocked on the door and nobody came. The door was not locked so they entered and asked Mr Fox for a specimen of his breath. He refused and was arrested and taken to the nick where he then provided the specimen after being requested to do so, and was found over the limit. The court said that the police officers had no right to enter Mr Fox's home as they had no reasonable cause to think that an accident had occurred which involved injury to another person and had not been reported as required by law. Thus they were trespassers and as such could not make the defendant take a breath test. *However*, although Mr Fox had been wrongly arrested this did not alter the incontrovertible evidence that he was over the limit and it was concluded he had been properly convicted. As the law stands now, however a breath test is taken (whether lawfully or not) 'in all cases it shall be admissible as evidence' (except, I assume, when the constable is not wearing his helmet ...).

Reference in the course of the Fox case was made to an earlier case Morris v. Beardmore (1980). In that particular case the facts were very similar. The police had followed the driver to his home. They knocked on the door and were let in by the driver's son. His father was in bed upstairs and refused to come down giving a message through his son asking the police to leave. The police went upstairs, invited him to undergo a breath test and when he refused they arrested him.

In a recent and well publicized case, although the defendant was below the legal limit when breathalysed he was still prosecuted, on the grounds that in the time that had elapsed between driving and the test his body had metabolized the alcohol that was then in his body — and they called scientific evidence to show that when he was driving his blood alcohol level was probably nearly twice the limit. Lawyers are very worried about this case, since it translates scientific probability into legal certainty.

TAXI CABS
There are about 14,000 taxi cabs in London and 6,000 elsewhere but taxi drivers don't come very high in my list of friends of the human race. I have very rarely seen a cabbie standing up and have come to the conclusion that several of them suffer from haemorrhoids or cantmovemyarsis, being constitutionally unable to dislodge themselves from the driver's seat. Have you noticed that when you get into a cab in England the driver always seems to be looking the other way? In most other countries the taxi driver will get out when you flag him down, open the door for you and help you in with your bags. But these seem all too foreign courtesies for the London cabbie. Mind you, I have an open mind, and if any reader can send me a picture of a cabbie in an upright position holding the door open, or with your suitcase in his hand, I shall make a public recantation of my allegations.

And yet cabbies consider themselves members of a caring profession. If you are a motorist I shan't need to mention the solicitude of the cabbie — how to keep you mentally alert he will cleverly suddenly stop in front of you to pick up or put down a fare, often without signalling, or unexpectedly do a U-turn or pull out from the pavement, all manoeuvres carefully calculated to keep your adrenalin flowing.

Do I sound jaundiced? Well I am. Not for nothing were cabs called 'growlers' in Victorian times on account of the surly attitude of their drivers. I can rarely get a cab from my London club in Pall Mall to take me back to my practice in south London, just a distance of five miles. The last time I tried I was told firstly 'Just off to my dinner, guvnor', and secondly 'Gotta fill up with diesel'. The third time a cab stopped I jumped in and sat down and then asked the cabbie to take me to my office. He said he was going home in the other direction. I told him of my previous experiences. No go. He wouldn't move. I then thought I would enforce my legal rights. 'I'm a solicitor', I said, 'and you are obliged to accept me as a fare'. The cabbie then thoughtfully replied, 'I don't care if you're f...ing Prince Philip. Geddout my cab!' To my eternal shame I did and phoned for a mini cab, as I couldn't see the way clear — even if he had finally conceded the point — to engaging in a sociable discussion of the issues of the day and profiting by his views on the police, social security scroungers, etc, a ritual I always look forward to whenever I go by cab.

You may have read that two cabbies were fined recently for expelling passengers. One passenger was smoking, while the other was earnestly defending Arthur Scargill. Quite sound reasons, you may think, but where will this end? Next thing you'll be out on your ear for sucking a Polo mint because the driver is dieting, or reading *Woman*, because he is a misogynist. We must take action now before it's too late and all our liberties are eroded.

Well, what are our liberties and rights in the matter? Here are some of them.

1. Must a cabbie take you wherever you want to go? Generally, yes, in London, provided the journey is less than six miles from the pick-up point and its duration is less

than one hour. There are variations though throughout the country. In London, if it is over six miles you have to negotiate a price for the trip in advance and pay it, no matter what the meter says.

2.   Does a taxi have to stop when you hail it? No, even if it displays the 'For Hire' sign. And the driver doesn't have to accept you if you jump in just after he has dropped a fare.

3.   Once a taxi has stopped to pick you up must he accept you? Yes, but in London there are certain conditions: (a) the destination must be within the Metropolitan Police district and (b) the proposed trip must be less than 20 miles or take less than one hour. A driver can be fined up to £400 for refusing to accept you.

4.   What is the limit on the number of passengers he may carry? It depends on the number shown on the plate in the back. For London black cabs this is four, but for other taxis it is usually five.

5.   What about luggage? As long as it's not dangerous he must allow you in with it, even bicycles.

6.   Animals? At his discretion.

7.   If you agree, say at a taxi queue at a station, to share a cab, is this OK? Yes, and he must drop each of you off as you require. As to his fare, all he's entitled to is the cost of the total distance plus the fixed amount for each additional passenger. He is strictly not allowed to pick up any others en route without your permission, whether you are in the cab by yourself or sharing it with others.

8.   There is a notice in the cab saying 'Please don't smoke'. Can I? Yes, this is just a polite request which, if you wish, can be ignored. By the same token you can't tell a driver to put his fag out.

Now something about the taxi cab itself. We all know that its interior dimensions were designed to allow a man to sit in it without removing his top hat, or so the story goes. It can turn on the proverbial sixpence. It is covered by strict inspection and safety regulations. But, until recently, not so strict as to prevent children falling out by playing with the door handles since the doors open towards the front and not the back as in a private car. Once a door is slightly open, if the cab is moving along at a fast lick, wind pressure will whip the door fully open in a jiffy. Thankfully, new rules mean that all London cabs must have protected door levers, and signs demonstrating how to open the window. In addition, the driver can lock the doors from his seat, and a light indicates to him if any of the doors is not properly closed.

Perhaps the Public Carriage Office, the official Police body supervising the operations of taxi cabs, is more concerned for the moral protection of the passenger. Until very recently no rear-view mirrors were allowed in the front of the cab enabling the driver to see what was going on in the back. Even now the position in which they are fixed is rigorously controlled. And while cabbies are allowed to have personal radios in the front they must be fixed at a specified point. What is more, no cassettes of any kind may be played in case they feature unauthorized advertising material or turn out to be pornographic rather than phonographic, so much is it feared that both driver and fare may become corrupted by playing them. Heard any good pornographic cassettes lately? I haven't, inside or outside a cab.

However, in one important area of law the Public Carriage Office has achieved considerable substantial reforms. It is comforting to know that it is no longer necessary for cabs to carry a bale of hay or a bucket and spade to shovel up the manure of their non-existent gee-gees. But you get nothing for nothing in this hard world, and the age-old concession whereby cabbies could relieve themselves against the rear offside wheel of their hackney carriage has had to be withdrawn. I don't know whether this was because Firestone took exception to their tyres being treated in this way, but there it is.

LIGHTS

You are driving a car in the daytime and the police pull you up to test your lights. All the lights on the car are working with the exception of one side lamp. Are you in trouble? Yes, you are. In the case of Payne v. Harland it was held on appeal that any faulty lighting equipment on a car even in daylight constitutes an offence.

TOWING A CAR

You have been disqualified from driving and decide to sell your car. A friendly neighbour tells you he will give you a tow to the garage where you propose selling it. He tows you there. You sit in the driver's seat of your car and are pulled up for driving while disqualified. Were you 'driving'? Yes, you were. Because in the court's view the essence of 'driving' is the use of the driver's controls in order to direct the movement of the car, the method of propulsion being irrelevant. Now, what if you had a fixed tow bar?

ICE-CREAM VANS

A Mr Nolan was driving his car when he saw an ice-cream van on his offside, that is, on his right, on the other side of the road. There were three cars parked on his near side (the left hand side of the road) opposite the van. He slowed down to let a car through coming from the opposite direction, then accelerated to 15 mph whereupon a little boy, Andrew Kite, aged five, ran out from between the parked cars to get an ice cream on the other side. Mr Nolan couldn't stop in time. He knocked the boy down, badly injuring him. Who was to blame? Mr Nolan, Andrew or the ice-cream van? Or all three in varying proportions? The trial Judge was upheld by the Court of Appeal. He ordered no damages against Mr Nolan. It was entirely Andrew's fault. Or...?

IN YOUR STREET

PLAYING IN THE STREET
Say your kids are playing football or cricket in the street. It is a backwater but in the eyes of the law still a highway, that is, 'a way over which there exists a public right of passage' and 'right for all her Majesty's subjects at all

seasons of the year freely at their will to pass and repass without let or hindrance.' If they play their games to the annoyance of a user of the road they are guilty of an offence and liable to a fine of up to £10. Surely we don't want to encourage them to watch *Match of the Day* indoors.

COQ AU VIN
You live in a quiet residential back street and a chap parks his lorry outside your house and lives in it. He is quite a nice chap and doesn't make a nuisance of himself. Can you do anything about it? The answer is — not a lot. If the occupier is not a gypsy and he is not causing a nuisance, and the lorry is not a caravan, why not let him stay there? Or, like a famous politician (Tony Wedgwood Benn), let him kip down in your garden shed? On the other hand you could get on to the police to have a go at him for obstruction but this may be very difficult to prove.

MUSIC IN THE STREET
Say you are a nightworker and are woken up in the afternoon by somebody playing a guitar or trannie underneath your window. Can you tell the musician to go away? Yes, you can, and he must. But you can't just tell him to naff off. You must give the lady or gentleman a reason for wanting him to go, but it doesn't have to be for disturbing your beauty sleep. So if you can't concentrate on your pools while listening to Jimmy Young or whatever, provided you are reasonable he must go. If he doesn't you can read the Act to him. Not the Riot Act but the Metropolitan Police Act 1864 Section 1, which can require a street musician to depart from your vicinity 'on account of the illness and the interruption of the ordinary occupation or pursuits of the inmates of such houses, or for other reasonable or sufficient cause'.

DEAD SHEEP
In the country where there are lots of sheep some of them are sometimes knocked down and killed on the road. Can you get the local council to remove the carcass which may

almost be outside your front door? The short answer is you can't, and if you can't find the motorist who killed the animal you have got to dispose of the carcass yourself. If you are a bit squeamish about this I suggest you get in touch with your local undertaker.

HIT-AND-RUN DRIVERS AND UNINSURED DRIVERS

If you have ever been involved in an accident in which the guilty party did a vanishing trick or was uninsured, or gave you false particulars after stopping, you have my sympathy. You should know that there is a body called the Motor Insurers Bureau. It is not a government body but funded by the insurance industry.

If you get judgement against an uninsured defendant the MIB will pick up the tab. Or if you are knocked down by a hit-and-run driver, that is an untraced motorist, provided the case is proved, and the quantum (i.e. the amount) of damage is agreed either by the MIB or an arbitrator, again they will pick up the tab. If you are the uninsured driver, don't think you will get off the hook if the MIB pay compensation to the other party. They are not there to protect you and will go after you to collect the money they pay out. If you haven't got enough ready cash they can make you bankrupt.

But you must note that the MIB will only compensate you for 'death or bodily injury to any person caused by, or arising out of, the use of the vehicle on a road'. You will not get any compensation for damage to your car, even if it's a complete write-off. A bit hard on you, you say, and I agree. What is more, the MIB are exempt from any liability in a number of special cases, the most significant of which are:

1.   If you were a passenger in a vehicle, say a car of a friend, and you knew he was not insured, you will get no compensation from the MIB.

2.   If you were a passenger in a vehicle owned by the Crown, or involved in an accident with such a vehicle, again you are not covered by the MIB although 'the same benefits in respect of compensation will normally be

afforded by the Crown to the victim in such cases as if they were in an accident caused by a private vehicle *except where the victim is a serviceman or servicewoman whose death or injury gives rise to an entitlement of a pension or other compensation from public funds'.*

You see, it's even harder on members of the armed forces who certainly get a raw deal (See 'The King can do no wrong', page 183).

I stress again that compensation is only for death or bodily injury. I am very critical of the EEC, particularly when they want to change the colour of our passports or stop us using the word 'chocolate', but among all their nutty decisions there is one which has my whole-hearted approval and that is a move to make the MIB liable for vehicular damage, etc, as well.

ROAD ACCIDENTS

FLASHING YOUR HEADLIGHTS
If you drove a car today you probably flashed your lights or had them flashed at you, as a courtesy to say 'come on, you're OK', or 'thank you for letting me through'. Flashers beware. The Highway Code says these signals have only one meaning, just like sounding your horn. They are to let another road user, motorist or pedestrian, know you are there. It was initially held in Clarke v. Winchurch in 1969 that a bus driver who flashed his lights to let a car pass in front of him which collided with a moped was partly negligent. But on appeal it was held that his light flashings only meant 'come on as far as I am concerned' and he had no liability at all. And the motorist? He was also let off because he had been as careful as possible and only inched his way forward.

BECKONING CHILDREN OR ADULTS ACROSS THE ROAD
The same considerations apply. Say you stop to let some kids across (even maybe at a zebra crossing), you wave them over and they are knocked down by another car. Are

you to blame? You could be, depending on the circumstances. I never wave anyone across the road; I just stop and put my hand out to warn other traffic. Even if you are not legally liable for an accident you bear a heavy moral responsibility in my view — even if you think you are taking no chances. The car behind you may not see the kids and have no idea why you stopped.

WHAT IF YOU ARE BLIND OR DEAF?
Then you take your life in your hands when you cross the road. In Bourhill v. Young the Judge said: 'a blind or deaf man who crosses the traffic on a busy street cannot complain if he is run over by a careful driver who does not know of and cannot be expected to observe and guard against the man's infirmity'.

WHAT IF A PEDESTRIAN SUDDENLY RUNS ACROSS A ZEBRA CROSSING?
In Kozimor v. Adey (1962), a woman of 40 had done just this. The car was 15 yards away doing 25 mph and couldn't stop in time, knocking her down. The driver was found 25 per cent responsible and had to pay damages accordingly. Under the Pedestrian Crossing Regulations 1954 he had an absolute duty to approach the crossing 'at such a slow speed that he could stop in time to avoid any pedestrians however unexpected and however foolish'. Why didn't he have to pay 100 per cent? Because the woman's failure to take care for her own safety was the primary cause of the accident.

ROAD WORKS
You are a roadman working for the 'corporation' and very properly engaged on your work in the middle of the road under repair, and you are struck by a bus. Should you have maintained a look-out? No, the bus was held on appeal to be solely to blame (Henley v. Exeter Corporation).

WALKING AT NIGHT
Two friends were walking on the left hand side of an unlit

country road at night, taking up 4'6" of roadway where there was no pavement or footpath. A car hit them, killing one and badly injuring the other. On appeal, although it was argued that they had not observed the Highway Code in not walking on the right, the Judge said it was entirely the driver's fault (Parkinson v. Parkinson). As was ruled in another case, a breach of the Highway Code creates no presumption of negligence. In plain English, if you don't do what you ought to do under the Highway Code the other fella can't get at you for that alone.

MY CONCLUSIONS
You will see that the outcome of a lot of these cases is surprising, many of them being on the borderline, with the first Judge going one way and the Appeal Judges the other. Because one chap is let off in one case it doesn't mean another will get off in a similar case. Very few accidents are identical; in fact they can't be. Everything will hinge round the particular facts of the case and whether the parties were acting reasonably. While as Lord Reid said (A.C. Billings v. Riden) 'we must have regard to human nature' and 'a reasonable man does not mean a paragon of circumspection', the golden thread (as Rumpole might put it) of reasonableness runs through the history of British justice.

6

FAMILY

STERILIZATION

You are a woman, and after pondering the pros and cons you decide you want no more children and arrange to be sterilized. However, the surgeon does not make a proper job of it (in fact, it's a right cock-up) and some time later you give birth to a healthy baby boy. You already have four children and are pressed for living space, so much so that you have to build an extension to your home for the new arrival. You also have to give up your job to look after the baby or get a mother's help. Apart from damages for pain and suffering, should you also be compensated for the extra substantial expenses you are going to have in bringing up the child and for the extension to the house? The Judge didn't think so in the case of Mrs Udale in 1983, because, he said, it was highly undesirable that a child should learn that his birth was a mistake. It would be against public policy to contribute to these expenses. Logical? Search me. Surely when the child grew up he would hear all about the case anyway. The ruling seems to go against all the canons of contract law which allow damages for all losses flowing from the breach of agreement. A bit like letting the baby out with the bathwater, if you ask me.

VASECTOMY — IT'S DIFFERENT FOR A MAN

You are a man, and like Mrs Udale mentioned in the previous paragraph you and your wife decide you want no more children. You see the surgeon who explains the operation. Not only will it be final and you'll become sterile for ever, but you won't be able to reverse its effects if you change your mind afterwards. You go through with it and a few months later your wife finds she's pregnant. It's too late to have an abortion and soon a healthy child is born.

Can you get damages from the surgeon? The Judge said 'yes' to the plaintiff in 1984, a Mr Thake, and he got just under £10,000 for the birth and upkeep for the little girl born. He said:

1.   The surgeon, a Mr Maurice, had entered into a contract to produce a particular medical result and he had failed. He didn't warn Mr Thake that there was a remote chance he might regain his fertility (this actually happened because Mr Thake was a rare case of 'late recanalization').

2.   The surgeon was in breach of his warranty that Mr Thake would become irreversibly sterile.

3.   Furthermore, his failure to warn Mr Thake was a breach of the duty of care he owed him as his patient.

4.   It was not against public policy (a common cop-out in the courts) to give an award of damages for the birth of a healthy child. The state policy of birth control meant that the birth of a baby was not always a blessing.

5.   However, no damages could be given for distress, pain and suffering by the parents since that was cancelled out by the joy received from the child.

6.   But they should get compensation for the costs of the child's birth and upkeep until her seventeenth birthday, which he set at £9,677.

The surgeon appealed against this decision in December 1985, and the Court of Appeal not only dismissed the appeal but in addition awarded another £1,500 to Mr and Mrs Thake for distress, pain and suffering, for which the original Judge had said they could not be compensated.

Now this ruling has far-reaching implications for all patient/doctor relationships. If your GP says 'Take these pills, they'll make you better', and they don't, can you claim damages against him? The first Judge in the Thake and Maurice case observed his decision would be regarded with alarm by surgeons and it seems doctors will have to be much more careful in future what they tell you.

VOID MARRIAGES

While we are on the subject of marriage, there are five distinct grounds on which your marriage may be totally void, i.e. it will be regarded as never having taken place. But you may still get financial compensation by way of maintenance payments if found necessary even though there was never any marriage at all in the legal sense. There is no time limit for asking the courts to declare a marriage void. These are the grounds:

1. *Family affinity.* You can't have relations with your relations. You mustn't 'marry' within the 'prohibited degrees' of relationship, or, in other words, if sex with your partner would amount to incest. Well, that's clear. An Act was passed in 1986 relaxing the law banning marriage between those related only by marriage, such as in-laws and step relations. However, various conditions and stipulations mean that it is still a complex issue; for example, a man can only marry his mother-in-law so long as his wife and his father-in-law are dead.

2. *Under age.* You must both have reached the age of 16 if one of you is domiciled in England (i.e. has his or her home here, basically), even if the marriage takes place abroad in a country where you can legally marry under this age. Such a marriage is void here as was the case in 1945 when a Hungarian girl aged 15 married a British citizen in Austria. By both Hungarian and Austrian law the marriage was valid but the wife got a decree of nullity here.

But if you are under 18 and get married you need the consent of your parent(s). If you don't have it and say you are over 18, or forge it, the marriage is still valid, but you have committed a criminal offence.

3. *Marriage formalities not observed.* If the formalities of the marriage itself as set out in the Marriage Act 1949 were not complied with the marriage may be void in certain circumstances.

4. *Bigamy.* Well, this speaks for itself. Of course, bigamy is a crime and while a learned Judge once said that the penalty for bigamy was two mothers-in-law, you may in addition get several years behind bars. The odd thing about bigamy is that you can often get off the *criminal* charge if seven years have passed since the first marriage with no news of your partner. This happened with sad

frequency during the war when servicemen were reported missing. Even if seven years have not gone by, you can still get off the hook if you had an honest belief that at the time of your second marriage your first husband or wife was dead. You don't have to prove that you knew your partner was dead: the *prosecution* has to prove that you knew your first partner was alive at the time of your second marriage. Which makes life quite a bit easier.

5. *The parties are not male and female.* In Alan Bennett's *An Englishman Abroad* the main character says to the heavily built (female) stage-door keeper of the Bolshoi Theatre in Moscow that she reminds him of a stoker he knew in the Navy. Make sure that when you marry you know for sure who or what your partner is.

In 1963 a well known model at the time called April Ashley went through a form of marriage with a Mr Corbett. Only she had been born a man and had undergone a sex-change operation consisting of the removal of the male paraphernalia and the formation of an artificial vagina. All to no avail. The marriage was declared null and void in 1970. I seem to remember this also happened to the 'marriage' of the son of the Chief Scout some years ago, Lord Rowallan. He obviously wasn't prepared.

So do be careful. Have a good look. In the daylight. Remember the German proverb *Bei Nacht sind alle Katzen grau* (At night all cats are grey).

THE CEREMONY ITSELF, OR 'OPEN THE DOOR, RICHARD' (POPULAR WARTIME SONG)
Are you married? If so, think back and try and remember whether the doors of the church or registered building or wherever you got married were open during the ceremony, because if they *weren't* you may be in trouble according to the law. The Marriage Act 1949 states quite specifically that the ceremony must take place between 8 o'clock in the morning and 6 o'clock in the evening — all that's quite clear, although it can happen that if a lot of weddings are scheduled your own ceremony may get delayed quite a bit. What is more important is that the doors should be open.

I have reflected for some time on what these words mean. Some registrars have told me that 'open' means 'unlocked'. But I think the usual meaning of 'open' must be given to this term. If I come in from shopping with my wife and say 'keep the door open' I don't mean 'keep it unlocked', I mean what I say. As to the *reason* why they must be kept open, I imagine this is either to give the bride or bridegroom a last chance to run for it, or to allow anybody to come in at the last minute (I seem to remember this was the case in *Jane Eyre*) and announce to all and sundry that the marriage cannot take place because of some lawful impediment. It might be that the bride was out of her mind (literally) to be getting married to that deceptively good-looking Adonis. Or Mr Adonis' wife might want to come along and tell the young lady that her swain was already married. And as we have seen, bigamy is a serious offence.

I like to think that we had literary MPs when the Marriage Act was drafted who took Shakespeare's words seriously, namely, 'Let me not to the marriage of true minds admit impediments'.

CHANGING YOUR NAME

Many people think this is a complicated process and you have to go through a lot of red tape. Not so. You don't have to put anything in writing at all because you can go under any name you choose, — even your next door neighbour's, or Rambo — provided you don't do this for fraudulent purposes, simply by using it.

In 1985 a market trader up North put the name of Harrods on the canopy over his stall. The well-known emporium got quite shirty when the news reached Knightsbridge and applied successfully for an injunction to stop this unheard-of presumption. I say 'unheard-of' advisedly because the sign had been up for seven years before Harrods got to hear about it, as I was told by Harrods' press officer, Miss Charmaine Graham-Taylor.

Not so long ago the Law Society conducted an advertising campaign to show the public what clever chaps we solicitors are and chose Mr Whatsisname as the name of the know-all barrack room lawyer, the duff gen merchant who diverted simple souls from seeing the experts. For some reason this miffed a law lecturer by the perfectly respectable name of Reynolds who promptly changed it to Mr Whatsisname. I found the logic of this step rather obscure. Presumably it was to heap ridicule on the uneasy heads of our professional masters — quite an ancient custom. I think he was successful for the campaign was never continued and both Mr Whatsisnames sank into oblivion.

And there is also the story of the patriotic civilian who was so inspired by the performance of a subaltern at the relief of Mafeking that he changed his name so it was the same as the subaltern's. The eponymous young cavalry officer was a chap called Baden-Powell who later founded the Boy Scout movement. So there are now several Baden-Powells around who are not strictly of the line. Interesting thing about the original B.-P. was that *his* father had named him after Robert Stephenson (these were B.-P.'s Christian names), who designed the first railway locomotive with his dad, George Stephenson.

There's quite a romance in names, even in ostensibly prosaic ones like Schnabel, Roosevelt, and Helena Rubinstein, who produced such delectable perfumes. Though I imagine if you were to create a new scent today you wouldn't follow her example and call it Essence of Cynthia Rappaport. I had a friend in the RAF who had come over from Germany just before the war. His name was Mordechai Zilbermann. When he got demobbed and settled here, he thought his name was a bit exotic for the locals and should be anglicized. So he had two sets of visiting cards printed, one lot saying 'Mordechai Zilbermann' (with two ns) and the other 'Mordechai Zilberman' (with just one n). The second lot, he said proudly, was 'for mein Englisch frenz'. Perfectly true, in substance anyway — I've changed *his* name slightly to avoid any embarrassment.

It was said in the papers at the time that Mr Whatsisname had changed his name by 'deed poll' as though there were some indefinable magic in these words. There ain't. A 'deed', if I may remind you, is just a document with a seal (nowadays a seal is just a little red sticker) alongside which you write your name. 'Poll' has nothing to do with parrots. It is an old word meaning 'to cut evenly' and just refers to the way the document used to be cut at the top to distinguish it — a document made by *one* person — from an 'indenture' — a document made by *two* persons — which was literally 'indented', i.e. cut zig-zag across the top. This was not for decorative purposes. When two parties, say a buyer and a seller, wanted to put a binding agreement in writing, an indenture would be drawn up and then cut in two halves in zigzag or wavy fashion, one half being kept by the buyer and one by the seller so that later in case of any dispute they could be matched up exactly to show that the parts belonged to each other irrefutably. A bit like Arthur Daley cutting a £50 note in half and giving one half to Terry with the promise of the other half when the job was done.

But you don't need a deed poll at all to change your name though a bank or a government department won't recognize your new name if you don't have some official evidence of it.

Anybody can give himself a title without waiting 50 years for it to be bestowed and going through the nail-biting rigmarole of being selected by the Prime Minister for ennoblement. If you want to call yourself Lord or Lady Mistletoe you can, provided you don't do it with fraudulent intentions. A bit barefaced but not against the law. There is a well-known persistent Parliamentary candidate who goes by the name of Screaming Lord Sutch, who formed the Monster Raving Loony Party. I believe he is quite respected in political circles by MPs who beat him at the polls.

Can you change the name of your children? Yes, you can, but you must normally have the consent of the father if the child is legitimate. If otherwise only the mother can change it, and she can do so, if she wishes, to the name of the father. He cannot object.

The 'Duke and Duchess of Streatham' at home

Now here's an anomaly. All I have said really applies only to surnames. The legal machinery to change your *Christian* name if given in baptism is very cumbersome. It has been held that a Christian name can only be changed by an Act of Parliament or by a bishop at confirmation (Vaisey, J. 1946). If you haven't been baptized you can do whatever you like.

Finally, your dirty weekend. There is one special circumstance when without really intending to commit a fraud you can be had up for passing yourself off under another name. That is, ladies and gentlemen, when you book in at a hotel under the *nom de plume* of Mr and Mrs Smith, or whatever, so that your weekend in Brighton can pass without incident. You will then be breaking the law. What law? It is Regulation 4 (1) of the Immigration (Hotel Records) Order 1972 made under Section 4 (4) of the Immigration Act 1971 which seemingly applies to everybody over the age of 16 whether or not they are immigrants. Under the Order you must supply details of your full name and nationality on booking in. The maximum penalty for not doing so is six months in the cooler plus a fine of £500.

Why not stay at home and settle down with a good book, something you've always meant to read such as, say, *Paradise Lost*? Could be quite appropriate.

HM THE QUEEN

You may at some time or other have written to Her Majesty to congratulate her, or more likely to bring to her notice some act of injustice, and invariably you will receive a gracious letter in reply from one of the Palace staff.

But did you know that quite unsolicited by you, if your friends make the right arrangement, a letter will arrive at your door from Her Majesty, no matter who you are and where you live, provided you meet one condition — and that is to reach your hundredth birthday. Every centenarian on that special day receives a personal message from Her Majesty. There is no statutory obligation for the Queen to send these messages but it is a royal custom hallowed by ancient usage. Well, not exactly ancient. The Palace tells me the custom started in 1917. At least that is as far as their records go back. It used to be a telegram until a few years ago but when the Post Office, as it was then, stopped the service, Her Majesty began to send a special letter called a tele-message.

So if you cherish a missive from the Monarch, stop smoking that cigarette, drinking that Scotch, and doing whatever turns you on but damages your health. Even if you don't last to be 100, at least you'll feel you're 100.

WILLS

WHY YOU MUST MAKE ONE

You must make a will. There are many reasons why you should. If you are married or have a lot of relatives you can spell out your wishes exactly and avoid heartaches for your nearest and dearest when you go. Even if you are alone in the world except for some long-lost cousin in Australia why not provide for close friends or — if you have none — for your dumb chums through the RSPCA or another charity? But be careful. If you do decide to leave money to the Australian cousin and he can't be found, all your money goes into limbo and will be frozen in some bank or building society until he is found. If he is not found the money remains there, as it does in a number of accounts in every solicitor's practice, until proof of the life or death of the beneficiary is established, which may be never.

If you die without making a will and have no next-of-kin whatsoever do you know what happens to all your property however large or small it may be? It is deemed to be *bona vacantia*. This means property nobody has any entitlement to, along with treasure trove, flotsam and jetsam found on the beach and waifs and strays (which mean stolen objects thrown away by a thief in flight and ownerless tame animals respectively) and goes to the Crown, that is Her Majesty The Queen.

Don't think it doesn't happen. The Treasury Solicitor, who administers these funds, told me the other day of a little old lady who died in 1985 leaving half a million, with no will nor family. It all went to the Crown. By now you are lifting up the telephone to call your solicitor to make a will. If you prefer to do-it-yourself with one of the forms you can buy at the stationers' be very, very careful since I feel the last thing in your mind will be to make lawyers rich (or Richer). And this is exactly what could happen if the complex formalities are not scrupulously observed.

If, on the other hand, you are doing nothing of the kind, please let me give you one last very compelling reason why you should make a will. This has to do with the bogeyman of our time, the tax man. I am, of course, thinking of what used to be capital transfer tax, previously known as death duty or estate duty in the old days. You may quite reasonably think that since your estate will be well below the figure at which this tax starts to run you needn't worry about this. But you should. In 1977 a Mr Paul Tegerdine, a 30-year-old haulage contractor, was killed in a car crash and when the case finally came to court in 1984, was awarded damages of £322,000. Mr Tegerdine died after the car driven by his wife Daphne was involved in a collision on the A471 in Norfolk. At the time of his death his two children were 15 and 11. Mr Tegerdine had not made a will and you would have thought that all his money should have gone to his widow for the benefit of herself and the children. But all Mrs Tegerdine got out of it was £25,000 and a life interest in half the remainder of the money, the other half going in equal shares to the children. This was because he died intestate (i.e. without making a will) leaving a wife and children. When this happens the law is that the widow gets a certain fixed sum — not the whole of it — and the children get the rest. Well, you may say, that's not so bad since the family received all the money one way or another. They didn't. The bogeyman in the form of the Inland Revenue entered the picture and took a hefty chunk in CTT out of the money due to the children.

Capital Transfer Tax has now been abolished and has been replaced with Inheritance Tax which is paid, on a rising scale, on gifts made after death (or in the last seven years before death), over a cumulative total of £71,000. The exemption for spouses still exists — as do the rules for the division on intestacy between children and surviving spouses. In Mr Tegerdine's case, although he left no will, under the rules of intestacy the children benefited and in the eyes of the tax man this benefit was deemed to be a disposal or transfer for the purposes of (what was then) CTT.

WHAT HAPPENS WHEN YOU GET DIVORCED?
If you are married and make a will leaving everything to the missus and then get divorced, what happens? Well, until 1982 the will stood. She would still get the lot, even though she was living with, or even married to, her fancy man and you were only a dull glint in her eye. The law has now changed. She gets nothing. In the quaint language of the law she is deemed to have predeceased you. She is cut off in all senses of the word. There is an interesting twist: say she had children (from your or another marriage) and you left these children or stepchildren a lot of money and then got divorced and the kids put up two fingers and went off with their mum. Those legacies are not affected and they collect. Why get divorced? Is it worth the hassle?

LORD JUSTICE HOMER NODS
It's an old saying that cobblers go around with holes in their shoes. And it's remarkable that some of the greatest writers of text books on wills died intestate. Furthermore the cases are legion of famous Judges over the centuries whose wills were defective. There is a text book in every solicitor's office called *Tristram and Coote's Probate Practice* which has gone through 24 editions. It is the lawyers' bible to which resort is had whenever a lawyer is presented with a testamentary teaser. One of the authors, Dr Tristram, however, left a will which was imperfectly executed and thus invalid.

In Victorian times a famous Lord Chancellor, Lord St Leonards, the Lord Hailsham of his day, was so proud of his will, it is said, that he used to get his daughter to read it to him every night in bed (only *he* was in bed, of course)

before he went to sleep (you must understand that Horlicks wasn't around then). Unfortunately, when he finally sank into his eternal slumber the will could not be found. But his daughter, poor girl, was able to recite it to the court by heart. Her testimony was considered unimpeachable and the will was duly proved, that is, probate was granted, even though the will was never produced, so creating a precedent to this day for oral testimony to stand when a will is lost.

Keep your will where someone can find it, preferably with a bank or a solicitor. And if you can't sleep at nights try reading the Law of Property Act 1925.

RICHER'S ADVICE TO THOSE ABOUT TO GET MARRIED
You don't have to be married to make a will. But if you are single, widowed or divorced and make a will and then get married anytime afterwards, the will is automatically revoked — unless you made it clear in your will that you were marrying a specific person and wanted the will to stand. So don't tie the knot until you have tied up your will carefully.

DIVIDING YOUR PROPERTY
What is the best way of sharing your favourite things between two children or friends who may fall out about who gets what? If you don't do it right the beneficiaries may say nasty things about you when you are dead and gone and make your ears burn. Of course, your ears may be burning anyway along with the rest of you. Why not simply say in your will that Jack should divide the stuff up into two halves and Jill should pick the half she wants. You see, where there's a will there's a way.

BEARING WITNESS — AND FORBEARING
Witnessing a will can be dodgy. An executor is the person you name to administer your estate and a beneficiary is someone who gets something given to him by your will. A lot of people think an executor must not witness your signature on your will. This is not so. Both an executor

and beneficiary can witness your will. In fact almost anybody can unless they are blind but a beneficiary will lose any benefit given to him by the will. Any gift made to a witness is invalid. But the will itself otherwise remains quite in order. An executor will never lose out on his executorship. But if he is also a beneficiary and witnesses the will it's curtains for him. If you leave something to your daughter, and your son-in-law witnesses the will she's had it too. The wife or husband of a witness cannot benefit from a will.

However, where a gift is left 'on trust' the beneficiary can still be a witness; this is quite complicated and gifts such as these should never be made without the assistance of a solicitor.

So unless you are leaving your money in trust, tell your kids to stand well away.

BENEFICIARIES WHO DIE BEFORE YOU
If you leave, say, £20,000 to somebody who dies before you, the money does not go to his or her estate, nor next-of-kin. It is said to lapse and goes to the person named in your will to get the residue of what's left after all your debts and other legacies have been paid. This person is called the residuary legatee. There is one important exception. If you leave anything to your son or daughter, or their children, and he or she dies before you, the gift does not lapse but goes to the 'issue' (i.e. children or grandchildren, etc.) of the beneficiary. Have I made the issue clear?

GRAVE MATTERS
This is a creepy subject and if you've got heartburn just now or are of a nervous disposition, skip this section and read the chapter on Leisure. Burials and deaths don't give me the creeps as my father was an undertaker, if not a very successful one, and I was brought up in the ambience of coffins, funerals, and shrouds which my aunts used to make to help out with their meagre income in the thirties. My dad didn't have a car but used to borrow a hearse and take my brother and me as kids down to the cemetery on a

Sunday afternoon, where we had great fun pulling each other round the grounds on the bier and generally larking around among the gravestones. (I believe even today quiet cemeteries are favourite trysting places for young lovers.)

Are you shocked? We took it all in our stride. Since childhood cemeteries have fascinated me, and there is much evidence of their same fascination for English writers from Gray ('Elegy Written in a Country Churchyard') to Jessica Mitford (*The American Way of Death*) and Evelyn Waugh (*The Loved One*) in our own day. Karl Marx is buried round the corner from me in Highgate cemetery and I have visited the graves of Heine and Oscar Wilde in Paris, Keats in Rome, Rupert Brooke on the Greek island of Skyros, and Thomas Mann (the German literary genius of the twentieth century) and James Joyce, both in sad cemeteries near Zurich in Switzerland. All great men buried, by a twist of fate, far from their homeland. It is always quite an experience to see their last resting place — one which reaches, in Godfrey Smith's words, a high tingle quotient.

Anyway, let me defer to your sensitivity and come down to earth and run through a dozen things you may like to know.

1. If a tombstone falls on top of you when visiting a cemetery it is a monumental piece of negligence on the part of the mason and you can recover damages from him as was the case in Brown v. Cotterill, when the Judge said 'a tombstone properly erected ought to stand for at least thirty years without repair'. This reminds me of the Yorkshire story of the man who wanted the words 'She was thine, O Lord' inscribed on his wife's tombstone. The mason left the 'e' off 'thine' so that it read 'She was thin, O Lord'. The client remonstrated with the mason who immediately agreed to rectify his mistake and put in an 'e'. When the client visited the cemetery a week later he saw that the inscription now read: 'E, she was thin, O Lord'. The other tombstone story I like concerns a Mr Longbottom who died prematurely as a young man. His epitaph read: *Ars longa, vita brevis*.

2.   If someone who had died said or wrote in his will that he wanted to be buried or cremated his or her relatives are not *legally* bound to observe these wishes. No person can make a binding disposition of his own dead body.

3.   You have a common law right to be buried in your parish churchyard or burial ground, if there is one, and it's not full. This was recognized as far back as 1794 in the case of Maidman v. Malpas. The right extends to non-Christians who had their home in the parish.

4.   If a clergyman wrongly refuses to bury you he is subject to an absolute suspension from the Ministry for three months (Cooper v. Dodd). When a clergyman thought the deceased was drunk when he died and didn't give him the benefit of the full burial service he likewise had to be suspended (R. v. Todd).

This by the way has nothing to do with the phrase 'benefit of clergy', which originally meant the exemption of clergymen from criminal trials and came to apply to all men and women who could read and preferred to be tried by the far more lenient church courts. Mere laymen could have the benefit only once, and were branded on the thumb to show they had had it. The words they had to read to prove their literacy were always the same — the first verse of Psalm 51 in Latin. In English this verse is 'Be gracious to me, O God, in thy true love; in the fullness of thy mercy blot out my misdeeds', and it came to be known as the neck verse by which criminals literally saved their necks. Of course, the Arthur Daleys in Shakespeare's time memorized the verse and recited it while pretending to read it. This nonsense came to an end in 1827, you will be pleased — or perhaps sorry — to hear.

5.   If somebody dies of a notifiable disease such as green monkey fever (!) or some types of food poisoning, etc, you mustn't hold a wake over the body. This is specifically prohibited by the Public Health Act 1936 Section 165.

6.   Nobody can own a dead body — the law does not recognize any *property* in a corpse, so it can't be stolen. But in 1613 in Haynes' case it was held that when a shroud

was stolen (Burke and Hare, where are you?) the thief could be charged by the original owner of the winding sheet.

7.   Does the doctor who certifies the cause of death have to see or examine the body? No, he doesn't — just as there doesn't have to be a corpse to prove murder. Provided he attended the person who died during his last illness recently, he can issue a certificate.

8.   A story has been going round for years that Quakers are buried vertically (i.e. standing up) but the Librarian of the Society of Friends assures me that this is a popular fallacy. Mind you, I think it is quite a good idea and would increase the capacity of our crowded cemeteries no end.

9.   There are strict rules against the erection of buildings on disused burial grounds. The word 'buildings' has caused a lot of legal controversy. For instance, you can build a toolshed but *not* an underground chamber for an electricity transformer, or a columbarium (pigeonhouse to you), bandstand, or *urinal* — as somebody wanted to do in Bermondsey in 1926.

You know, death stares you in the face in the most unlikely places. If you have ever been to Regent's Park near London Zoo you may know the secret garden (open to the public) by St John's Lodge. When you come up to the Inner Circle from Cumberland Terrace and turn right you will find it on your right — for me the most beautiful and private rose garden in the world. To get into it you pass a little gate lodge and just beyond it there is a largish carriage house, or garage, as I thought. This seemed an ideal summer house to write my books — very nicely tiled inside — and I rang up the Department of Environment to see if I could rent it. Sorry, they told me, the whole place has just been sold. It was a *mortuary* built by the Marquess of Bute who lived there at the turn of the century. He was of a religious turn of mind and had also built three chapels, one underground. The mortuary was for his private use. I am willing to lay even money that nobody living in those marvellous Nash terraces in Regent's Park knows that if they had been quick off the draw they could have converted a mortuary and lived there communing with the spirits of Bute. There's oneupmanship for you.

10.   Are cemeteries contagious? Not really. Though in 1878 the Amersham Burial Board had to pay damages to a farmer whose cattle died after eating the poisonous foliage of yew trees overhanging his land from the cemetery. Be careful none of the kids next door have a nibble at your yew trees if you've got any because the same thing could happen to yew, wherever.

11.   Cremation is quite popular nowadays. Except in Israel where it is taboo on religious grounds. Where in the world are most people cremated (excluding India, where it is traditional, and China, where it compulsory)? In Japan, where in 1980 91 per cent of the dead population went this way. Where the least? Not the USA, even though the figure was only 10 per cent (we all know the loved one is often embalmed by the local mortician, made up and laid to rest in a satin lined coffin). It is France, where the figure is just 1 per cent. Only 4,500 were cremated there in 1980 contrasted with 421,000 in Great Britain (64 per cent).

12.   If after reading all this you would rather be buried in your own back garden, you may be. In 1984 a garage proprietor in Cornwall buried his aged aunt in a meadow he owned. Evelyn Waugh and his wife were both laid to rest in a field adjoining their house, now the home of their son Auberon Waugh. And Lord Beaverbrook buried his first wife in the garden of his country house, Cherkley in Surrey, and according to *The Sunday Times* would sometimes gaze out of his window and say in a mournful voice, 'There lies goodness'. All you have to do is observe the local by-laws and notify the council within four days of the interment. I rang up both the Planning Department in Camden, where I live, and the Environmental Health Officer, to ask their requirements. The latter had never been asked this question and couldn't answer it. The former couldn't either and said rather lugubriously: 'Well, it might be classified as minor engineering works for which you would need planning consent'. Both said they would look up the point and ring me back. Neither did.

7

WORK, BUSINESS, AND CONTRACTS

REFERENCES

What can you do if your boss won't give you a reference? Not a lot. What is more if he does send one to your prospective employer but says all sorts of things about you which you think unfair you can do absolutely nothing about it, unless the reference includes recklessly untruthful errors of fact or is malicious. You have no automatic right to a reference at all, and if one *is* given you have no right to see it even if it costs you the new job. So don't call your boss a wally when you leave him. Otherwise you may turn out to be the wally. And did you know you are not entitled to any holiday pay unless your contract of employment says so? You have no automatic right to be away and be paid for it, even on Bank Holidays. It's a hard life.

UNFAIR DISMISSAL

You are suddenly given the sack for no justifiable reason. All your friends and the Citizens Advice Bureau tell you to go to an Industrial Tribunal for compensation, which you do. Will you get it? You had been working for your boss for several years without complaint and the sacking was completely unfair. A friend of yours was in the same boat only last year and got £2,000 from a Tribunal. I have to tell you that however strong your case is it may not depend on the facts of the dismissal. It could depend on how you were paid. Not *how much* you were paid but *how* you were paid. What's that got to do with it, you say. Quite a lot. You probably heard of Peter Stringfellow's London nightclub, The Hippodrome. One of his employees was a bouncer, a Mr Saeed Abdalla, known as Big Max, whose job it was to prevent undesirable visitors to the club. He was a sort of minder, a Terry McCann. According to him

113

he had to make sure that entry was denied to blacks, fatties, Cockneys and 'squares'. He performed his duties admirably but with perhaps an excess of zeal. His boss said that he threw a woman across the street, felled a Chinese with one blow (a kind of Big Max takeaway), and insulted rich club members, including Mr Steel the Liberal leader, who I think we would all agree is neither a black, fattie or Cockney.

Big Max said it was all lies. But a Chelsea Tribunal on 17 December 1985 didn't even bother to look at the contradictory claims of the parties. It came out that Big Max had been in the habit of taking 'readies' in the hand every week from his employers as part of his remuneration, which he somehow neglected to enter in his annual tax return. In the eyes of the tribunal, reflecting the current outlook of HM Inland Revenue, this was very naughty. Big Max was, in the language of the law, party to an illegal contract, i.e. his contract of employment wasn't worth the paper it was written on.

So if your boss gives you some crinklies every week, take care. You won't have a leg to stand on if you decide to sue him for redundancy money or unfair dismissal. And if you are the boss, you can always get rid of a troublemaker without it costing you a penny.

UNFAIR DISMISSAL ON GROUNDS OF ILL HEALTH

You're the boss. One of your employees is a chronic absentee due to ill health. You've been paying his wages while he has been away and although he has been with you for a long time you really feel that enough is enough. Can you sack him? Yes, you can but you must be very, very careful. First, you've got to see the employee and discuss the matter with him. Second, if there is any doubt whatsoever about the employee's medical condition you must find out the facts by getting a doctor's report, for example. You should ask the doctor for as much detail as possible regarding the employee's medical future including his ability to carry on working, taking into account the type of work he did, etc. It is most important to take medical advice. In the case of East Lindsey D.C. (1977) the boss sacked a diabetic and while it was ruled that he had grounds for doing so it was found that the employee had been unfairly dismissed because no proper medical advice had been obtained regarding the employee's condition, etc. Take particular care when you sack someone for being ill, otherwise you might be the one to end up feeling pretty sick.

UNFAIR DISMISSAL ON GROUNDS OF FIGHTING
AT WORK

The boss is usually quite within his rights to give you the boot if you get involved in a fight. This does not have to be laid down in black-and-white as a rule of management. But in two cases in 1984 it was held that the employer had acted unfairly when 1. a worker was sacked after a colleague pretented to square up to him and he butted him with his head and 2. a worker threw a cup of tea over another following a lot of legpulling and also got sacked for his pains. The moral of the story is: box clever and never tangle with the boss.

SO YOU WANT TO BE A COMPANY DIRECTOR

Many misguided people think there's a lot of cachet or prestige in describing themselves as company directors. They don't realize it's almost as dubious nowadays as a woman calling herself a model. But if you've really set your heart on it all you need is £85. This is about the going rate for a ready-made company in the UK and for this modest sum you can not only appoint yourself a director overnight but also become chairman of your very own limited company into the bargain. You can have as many companies as you like and as many directorships. The record was set in 1961 by Mr H.T. Nicholson who had over 450.

Another popular fallacy is that the expression 'limited company' confers some magic status on your operations with its connotations of city solidity and respectability and that it's far more impressive to call yourself Arthur Daley and Co. Ltd rather than just Arthur Daley and Co. Far from it. What it means for the unwary is that the liability of the shareholders in the company if it goes bust is limited to the amount of the company's capital which can in total be as low as £100, hence the expression 'a hundred pound company'. It can be far safer to deal with a company, i.e. a partnership or even a sole trader, whose liability is unlimited and who can be made bankrupt if he or they can't pay money owed to you. Incidentally, a company never officially goes bankrupt: it goes 'into liquidation' if it can't meet its commitments.

Now, company directors. You may think if you are one you have complete immunity from any penalties for illegal acts perpetrated by your company which you will rightly regard as a separate entity that 'has neither a soul to be damned nor a body to be kicked'. Wrong again. You can go to the clink and/or be fined *personally* anything from £50 to £2,000 with daily default fines on top for criminal offences committed by the company of which, if you are on the board of a largish company, you may not have the faintest idea. The prison terms you can expect range from two to ten years for false or reckless statements and returns and other contraventions of the relevant statutes. And that's only on the criminal side: there are a host of *civil* liabilities as well. For instance, in 1983 the DHSS recovered from the personal assets of directors over £1 million of National Insurance contributions their companies had failed to pay. Apparently the DHSS are having second thoughts about pursuing directors for this particular liability and it seems you may now get off the hook if your company hasn't paid these contributions. But even now, if you sign a cheque or an order for goods for the company and the company's fully registered name doesn't appear on the cheque or order form you will be personally liable if the company defaults, that is if the cheque bounces or the goods are not paid for. Many statutes do not require proof of criminal intent on your part. Where, under such legislation, an offence has been attributable to any consent, connivance or neglect on the part of a director, manager, secretary or similar officer, he *as well as the company* will be guilty of the offence.

If you would like to know about the personal liabilities of a director there is a very good 180-page guide produced by the Institute of Directors which anybody can buy for £5.95. It is called simply *Directors' Personal Liabilities*. You should also know there is new legislation on the way to make directors personally more accountable for the misdeeds of the companies they direct.

Who wants to be a millionaire?

VERBAL CONTRACTS

Many people think *all* contracts have to be in writing, for example you often hear people say 'he promised to buy my car or hi-fi or paint my kitchen and he didn't. But I can't do anything about it because it wasn't in writing.' You can. We are all entering into contracts every day by word of mouth. When we buy a beer, a newspaper or a carton of milk, board a bus or taxi or buy a ticket on the tube we enter into a contract imposing obligations on ourselves and the shopkeeper or London Transport or whatever. Of course, very often when you buy or order something you are asked to sign a document, for example by a travel agent in the case of a holiday, and this fleshes out the contract and states all the conditions. Even if you have only booked the holiday by telephone or in the travel agency without signing anything, you can still be forced to pay up, just as a cabbie can sue you if you don't pay his fare.

By law only very few types of contract must be in writing and these, except for consumer credit agreements (such as HP and loan agreements) are mainly very obscure and technical ones, such as bills of exchange, promissory notes and contracts of marine insurance. However, one very common kind of contract — that which is for the sale or purchase of land, houses or such like — has to be *evidenced* in writing. There usually *is* a written contract as such but there need not be. But if you want your legal rights following a verbal agreement when you buy or sell a house and the other party reneges, you have to show the court something in writing from him or her referring to the deal, and providing the letters you rely on are not marked with those magic words 'subject to contract' you're home and dry. The other party will have made a binding agreement and has to go through with it or pay substantial compensation.

Be very careful. If you fall in love with a house or flat you want to buy and feel it's the decent thing to confirm your offer of, say, £40,000 by a nice letter to the owner, always put in the letter (anywhere — top, bottom or in the middle) 'subject to contract'. If you don't and your surveyor later finds that the house is a bad buy at the price, you may still have to go through with it. And, by the way, once you have exchanged contracts to buy a house or flat, by a quirk of the law you theoretically become the legal owner and, if the house burns down or is damaged before you 'complete' whilst the man you are buying it from is still living there, you ordinarily still have to pay up on the completion date. So it is imperative that you insure the property as soon as you exchange contracts. I say 'ordinarily' because the one glimmer of light is that the seller has to look after the property until completion takes place. In 1981 a Mr Gorman moved out a week before completion. A frozen pipe burst and flooded the house. The buyer in this case got compensation because the Judge ruled that Mr Gorman should have turned off the water at the mains before leaving.

But don't trust to luck. Ensure that you insure.

WRITTEN CONTRACTS

'I DON'T UNDERSTAND ALL THIS LEGAL JARGON'
Say you sign a document without reading or understanding it carefully. It may be for the hire or purchase of a car, or the installation of a new kitchen, or a guarantee, and so on. After signing you take home a copy of the document, you settle down with a double Scotch and re-read it. You are disconcerted to see that it is not what you thought it was, or, as Eric Morecambe might have put it, 'never has your flabber been so gasted'. Can you recant? The short answer is 'no'. Provided it is not essentially different from what you thought you were signing and there was no misrepresentation by the other party you are bound by what you have signed.

In 1964 a Mr Galbraith hired a caravan. He thought he was buying it and signed what he thought was a hire-purchase agreement. But the agreement was just for hiring it. After some time he realized his mistake but it was too late and the owner repossessed the caravan keeping all the money Mr Galbraith had paid out in rent. An earlier case which may raise a hollow laugh from unkind readers involved a solicitor, a Mr Webb, who signed a deed thinking it was a conveyance. It wasn't. It was a transfer of a mortgage making Mr Webb liable to pay it. And the court ruled he had to.

What if you trust the person you are dealing with and sign a form with lots of blanks in it and hand it to him to fill in the details and the details inserted are not in accordance with your instructions? Generally, you can't renege. So don't do it.

IS IT A CRIME?
Do you think it could be a criminal offence *not* to put a contract in writing? Yes, it could. A fine of up to £400 can be imposed on anybody demanding payment for an entry in a commercial or trade directory if a written agreement has not been signed by the person dunned for the money. It's all in the Unsolicited Goods and Services Act 1971, which was passed following an epidemic in the 1960s of conmen publishing rogue directories listing names of tradesmen and businessmen who were later billed for this unwanted service.

SOME CURIOUS CONTRACT CASES
1.   In 1955 three ladies, A, B and C, who lived in the same house, used to enter a weekly competition run by a Sunday newspaper. The coupon was sent off in the name of B. One week they were lucky and won a lot of money, but B refused to give A any of her share. A sued B and won the case and her share of the money too.
2.   A Mr Lens won a competition at his golf club but the club refused to hand over his prize. He had done nothing legally untoward and sued for it. He lost the case because there was no contract between the parties: it was a 'social arrangement'. Poor Mr Lens was out of focus.
3.   Various disgruntled people who do the pools sue the pools companies from time to time. They always lose. Why? Because the agreement between the pools companies

and the punters is normally binding in honour only and has no legal consequences. As Falstaff said 'What is honour? A word. What is that word honour? Air. A trim reckoning.' But he wasn't complaining about his pools.

BEARDS — IN PURSUIT OF THE HIRSUTE

Are you a chap? Can you ever get into trouble if you grow a beard without a moustache or vice versa? I mean *legally*? If you are a Tory Cabinet minister your leader might give you a wigging if you did, since curiously Mrs Thatcher's entourage are, at the time of writing, wholly without facial fringes. If you are a clergyman you might worry what your bishop will think (seen any bishops with moustaches lately?) And if you are a waiter in a top hotel, etiquette decrees that your face must be hairless.

George Orwell noticed this in the thirties and it's still the same today. In *Down and Out in London and Paris* he wrote:

No one in the hotel wears a moustache, except the cooks. I should have thought you would have noticed it. Reason? There *is* no reason. It is the custom. I saw that it was an etiquette, like not wearing a white tie with a dinner-jacket, and shaved off my moustache. Afterwards I found out the explanation of the custom which is this: waiters in good hotels do not wear moustaches, and to show their superiority, they decree that plongeurs shall not wear them either; and the cooks wear their moustaches to show their contempt for the waiters.

Hair is quite interesting. In 1965 a Mr Richard Corson wrote a 700-page book on hair. And we all remember the musical, of course. But legally, you could be in trouble if you are in the armed services. They all take hair seriously and impose severe restrictions on your facial appearance. These are to be found in the Queen's Regulations for the Navy, Army and Air Force which have the force of law. For example, in Chapter 11 of the *Queen's Regulations for the Navy* there is a section headed 'Growth of Hair' which states:

When permission to grow a beard is given the use of a razor is to be discontinued entirely, as moustaches are not to be worn without the beard, nor the beard without moustaches except by non-continuous service Officers' Steward, Officers' Cook ratings [I wonder whether the chap who drafted these regulations was influenced by George Orwell] excluding Maltese who may wear their beards and moustaches or moustaches only or be clean-shaven as each may elect ... Hair, beards, moustaches and whiskers are to be neatly cut and trimmed, and ... uniformity in length is to be established.

So now you know. Mind you, I'm a bit sorry for Maltese cooks in the Navy. I suppose it is the (Maltese) cross they have to bear.

While we are on the subject of body decoration I urge you to consider tattoos for a moment, for if you are a chappess with a teeny weeny tattoo don't try and join the Army. They won't have you. Yes, this is perfectly true, and I quite understand how this can get under your skin. It was all brought to light by a plastic surgeon in a letter to The Times on 20 May 1985. I have heard of Beating the Tattoo, but this is ridiculous. Groucho Marx used to sing a song about 'Lydia, o Lydia, Lydia the tattooed lady', so there must have been some around in his time, which is admittedly going back a bit. My advice to such military aspirants is to form a ginger group and call themselves something snappy like LYDIA, an acronym for Liberated Young Daughters Intent on the Army, and get a grant from the local council.

8

LEISURE

PASSPORTS

Here is an easy way to win a bet. Ask a friend casually if he is willing to lay even money on how many times the words 'British Passport' appear in a passport apart from on the front cover. Well, I'll ask you. I'll make it easy — just say how many times there are to the nearest thousand. That's it, 'thousand'. It may come as a surprise to you that the words 'British Passport' are mentioned over 10,000 times — just under 12,000 to be more exact. They are printed in tiny block capitals in a House and Garden shade of eau-de-nil on every page, including the inside front cover, which makes 31 pages in all. There are about 80 lines (excluding the white band) on every page and on each line the words appear six times. So there.

And here's another bet you can try on your mate. You pay £15 for your passport (£22.50 if particulars of your spouse are included) so you would be quite right in thinking it belongs to you. Wrong again. If you look inside the passport on the very last page you will find the words '*Caution*. This passport remains the property of Her Majesty's Government in the United Kingdom and may be withdrawn at any time.'

And here's yet another one. If you are a married woman do you have to have a passport in your married name? You don't. But to avoid problems abroad, particularly if your driving licence or Access card or whatever is in your maiden name, you should carry with you a copy of your marriage certificate to confirm your change of name. Though how much impact this will have on a boarding-house keeper in Bucharest is another matter.

Now here's a little conundrum. You're a bride-to-be and you are going to Greece or Spain for your honeymoon. You already have a passport — or maybe you don't have a passport at all — but you want a new one in your married name. If you already have one in your maiden name it is not necessary to get a new one as you can continue to use the old one. Do you go to the Passport Office immediately after the marriage ceremony? Not at all. All the world loves a lover and the officials at the Passport Office are no exception. You can apply for a passport in your married name *before* you get married; it will be sent to the Church or registry office but will only be handed over after the ceremony. You mustn't use it before the wedding and must agree to surrender it if there is no marriage. Alternatively, if you travel on your existing passport you can get this altered later by sending the passport and your marriage certificate to the Passport Office who will amend it and return it to you with your new name. Or you can be included on a joint passport with your husband, and vice-versa, as can any of your children under 16, but you can only use it when accompanied by the principal holder. A wife or child can never travel alone on a passport issued to the old man for joint use.

Can you have *two* passports, I mean British passports, in the same name? You can. Some countries will refuse you entry if your passport shows you have visited certain other countries. Many Arab countries won't let you in if they see from your passport that you have visited Israel, for example. So you keep one for Israel and the other for Saudi Arabia.

What happens if you're on the way to the airport and suddenly realize you've left your passport at home and have no time to go back for it? Don't panic. You may be able to get an emergency travel document from the immigration office at the airport, particularly if you break down and cry. I'm perfectly serious. My ex-wife did this once and it worked like a charm.

I once went to the South of France with a girlfriend who left her passport at home. No trouble at all. At Heathrow they were very understanding and didn't even bother to issue any papers to her. When we got to Nice I explained to the immigration officer in my very best broken French what had happened, and he just waved us through. There's Gallic courtesy for you. But take care. If the *moules marinières* or *tripes à la mode de Caen* he had had for his lunch had been indigestible his attitude may not have been so 'gentil'.

You are an Englishman born and bred. Can you be refused a passport? You certainly can. If you are under 18 and want to travel against the wishes of your parents or guardian, or if a British warrant for your arrest has been issued, or you've been repatriated and haven't yet paid your fare (the Foreign Office used to call such persons officially, if somewhat masonically, 'distressed British subjects') or someone to whom granting a passport would be 'against the public interest' — if you are any of these you would be refused a passport. In fact, the issue of a passport is 'under the royal prerogative'.

Which brings me to some rather interesting legal lore. Inside the front cover of your passport you will find surmounted by the Royal Coat of Arms the following magisterial exhortation printed in formal copperplate like you find on invitations to the Queen's garden parties at Buckingham Palace and just as beautifully proportioned:

Her Britannic Majesty's
Principal Secretary of State for
Foreign and Commonwealth Affairs
Requests and requires
in the Name of Her Majesty
all those whom it may concern
to allow the bearer to pass freely
without let or hindrance
and to afford the bearer
such assistance and protection
as may be necessary.

Very Palmerstonian, very gunboat, but does it mean much? I am afraid not. About as meaningless as the statement on all £5 notes signed by the Chief Cashier of the Bank of England: 'The Bank of England promise to pay the bearer on demand the sum of Five Pounds'. This sad fact was judicially recognized in 1932 when it was held there were no legal means by which the Crown might be compelled to exercise its protection on behalf of a passport holder (China Navigation Co. Ltd v. A.-G.). Do you remember too, a couple of years ago our French friends refused entry to some gentlemen who were not altogether French in appearance at the Channel ports? Yes, they did. *And* they all had the necessary documents.

It has long been held that if you have a British passport giving you the protection of the Crown, such as it is, you likewise have a duty of allegiance to the Crown wherever you may travel. This may all sound rather academic but it didn't to Lord Haw-Haw, the British traitor hanged in 1946 (see page 175). It was the very argument put forward by the prosecution and accepted by the Judges — well, four out of five of them. He broadcast for the Nazis and because he was a holder of a British passport he was convicted and executed under the Treason Act 1351. Yes, 1351. That's not a printing error. So if you're planning to commit treason, surrender your passport first.

I have said that a passport can be refused on various grounds. There is no formal machinery for appeal or judicial review, which I think strikes at the roots of our democracy. They seem much more enlightened in the USA where you have a constitutional right to a passport (Kent v. Dulles 1958) and India, where it's held that the issue of a passport was recognized by Magna Carta, no less (Sawhney v. Assistant Passport Officer, Government of India 1967). Magna Carta, may I remind you, was the Great Charter of liberties extorted from King John in 1215. But there was no passport office then.

You very often hear of the police impounding a passport if they believe the holder has committed some crime and may flee the country. *They have no legal right to do so.* This was confirmed by the Court of Appeal in 1969 (Ghani v. Jones). The police may always take from you any documents, etc, that may be material evidence against you, but a passport doesn't come in that category, unless you are up for forging it, of course. However it can be a condition of bail that you surrender your passport. You do not have to do so, but you stay in the clink unless you do.

Another thing. Just as you've no legal right to a passport, the State has no legal right to prevent a British citizen from leaving or entering the country without a passport, as long as you have some document such as a birth certificate to prove who you are. The *Daily Telegraph* took this up in 1968 and as a test case sent one of its journalists, Mr Ian Colvin, to Heathrow to see if he could go abroad without his passport: he wasn't allowed to go and the case caused a rumpus. Mr Callaghan, the then Home Secretary, quoting the Aliens Order 1953, explained that Mr Colvin might have been thought to be an *alien* and the immigration officers were quite entitled to control the movements of aliens. I believe Mr Colvin was Scottish. Well, er ... I was under the impression we took in the Scots in 1707 by the Act of Union. Maybe the Scots felt they were taken in, too.

I still have a lot of blind spots about passports and rang the Passport Office to put my mind at rest. Correction: *tried* to ring them. I tried for three days and nobody answered.

I explained my predicament to a nice press officer at the Home Office. She gave me a number to ring — the same number I had already tried for three days. I didn't bother but I now know why Menotti, the great Italian composer of our day, wrote a whole opera called *The Telephone*. As far as I can remember the heroine couldn't make a connection and killed herself — or was it *The Consul*? Anyway, I'm afraid this does mean that I can't tell you:

1. the exact date when we're going to lose our blue passports and have them replaced by red ones, the result of another nutty EEC directive. You may well remember the outcry a couple of years ago when the Post Office, as it then was, started painting our cherished telephone boxes *yellow*. Luckily, they only got as far as the first three in Edgware Road near Marble Arch, which were still there until quite recently as a reminder of 'the insolence of office', or red tape, as you might call it.

2. why you've got to get an application form for one signed by 'a doctor, lawyer, police officer, MP, minister of religion or JP' who has known you for at least two years. It didn't stop John Stonehouse, the ex-Cabinet minister from getting one in a false name some years ago and doing a bunk to Australia. And talking of Stonehouse,

3. how he did it. It was said at the time that he prowled round cemeteries looking for someone with roughly the same date of birth on the tombstone and then applied in the corpse's name, and

4. why there is that strange white band on every page of your passport. Now that bugs me.

HOLIDAYS

LOSING YOUR LUGGAGE

A man flying to Paris with three suitcases went up to the check-in counter at Heathrow and said 'I'm flying to Paris but I'd like you to send one case to Rome, another to Lisbon and the third to New York'. 'I'm afraid we can't do that, sir' replied the airline rep. 'Why not?' asked the passenger. 'You did it last time.'

Leisure

Losing or even mislaying your luggage in transit is not only very irritating it can be quite expensive too. When you start adding up the contents of your bags you may be surprised at your own affluence. Even if you take out travel insurance you must read the small print carefully: does it

give you adequate cover on everything you're taking, including the cameras and other high value items? Is it just for replacement value, or new-for-old? You wouldn't be very happy if you only got £100 for your wife's holiday outfit which cost her £300 just a few months back. Is there an excess on the policy making you responsible for the first £25 or £50 of any loss? Have you kept the receipts? Or will it be your word against theirs? Did you make and keep a list of everything in the suitcases (I don't know anybody who does). It's very galling after your claim is finally met to remember you didn't put in for a couple of expensive pullovers.

Many people go on foreign trips, particularly business travellers, without taking out proper insurance for their baggage, if indeed they take out any at all. So what compensation do you get from the airline companies when they lose or mislay your luggage? Not a lot. Their liability is much less than you think. It is limited by the vagaries of the Warsaw Convention 1929 as amended by the Hague Protocol of 1935, an international agreement entered into by most of the airlines and embodied here in the Carriage by Air Act 1961. It deals with airlines' liability for death, personal injury, and loss, damage or delay to baggage, which is set at ridiculously low levels. The American authorities would have no truck with the Hague Protocol which it considered far too unprotective and devised their own formula for higher scales of compensation for all flights to or from the USA in the Montreal Inter-Carrier Agreement of 1966. If you read the small print on any UK flight ticket you will see that on all non-US flights the ceiling is either $10,000 or $20,000 for death or personal injury, depending on whether the airline was party to the Warsaw Convention or the Hague Protocol. For US flights it zooms up to $75,000.

Coming back to your luggage, the compensation you may get is not related to the *value* of what you lose but its *weight*. The current going rate is £13.80 per kilo of checked baggage. (This means that if you don't check in your weekend bag or briefcase you take with you on the plane, you are not covered at all.) Assuming you take 20 kilos (44 lbs) with you, which is pretty average, the most you'll get if the lot is lost is £280 — about the price of a good camera and a suit. The moral is obvious. Always take out insurance even if you go just for the weekend, and read the small print carefully. If you can't be bothered, ask for it to be explained to you.

How many of us went abroad in 1984? My guess was way out. Isabel, who is in charge of public affairs at ABTA (Association of British Travel Agents) gave me the figures — 15.3 million UK residents travelled abroad in 1984. And that's a lot of suitcases.

RENTING HOLIDAY HOMES ABROAD

You read in one of the Sundays an ad describing a dream home to let for your summer holiday in the South of France, or Italy, or Spain. The owner is also English. You see him and feel reassured enough to take it and sign the letting agreement which says 'In case of any dispute, English courts will have jurisdiction'. When you arrive at the cottage, villa or flat on the outskirts of Villefranche, or wherever, not only is there no sea view, nor swimming pool, as promised, but the place is running with cockroaches. In fact it's the pits. No dream, but a nightmare. When you get home, everybody tells you to sue the malefactor. You've got witnesses, taken photographs, and it's an open and shut case. Or is it?

You may think you're on to a winner in your local county court — but I'm sorry to tell you you'll have to think again. If you take it to court the case will be chucked out because the defaulting owner has a perfect defence to your claim. No English court (despite what the letting agreement says) has any jurisdiction to deal with it. It's all to do with the Common Market which seems to affect our lives in the most unexpected ways. The EEC Convention of 1968 to which our leaders have committed us has laid down that *you can only sue in the country where the property is situated.* And obviously to keep expenses down you would have to put your case before a court in the locality of the

'Oh God, Roger ...it's so peasant!'

property itself. Now English lawyers' fees are painful enough. But French lawyers' fees are enough to give you a migraine. What's more, unless you feel you can explain your claim adequately to the French (or Spanish etc.) lawyer yourself, you'll end up paying two sets of fees since you'll have to go through an English lawyer as well. Or even three or four sets of fees if you lose the case and costs are awarded against you, since the English owner will probably go through two lawyers like you.

The thought is now crossing your mind that in future you will take all your holidays in Broadstairs. So what do you do? Not a lot. But here's a helpful hint. If at all possible, always pay for your holiday — or even part of it — by credit card and let Visa or Access have the headache of sorting things out. As I have said earlier (page 11) the credit card companies — i.e. the banks — carry the can for almost any claim if you don't get satisfaction from the malefactor. In fact you can go straight to the bank without suing the wrongdoer.

I never did like all that sangria and paella and bullfighting anyway.

SPORTING EVENTS
I think useful research could be done on the impact of games and sports on the English language. We are a very sporting nation — literally, vicariously, and figuratively. The battle of Waterloo was won on the playing fields of Eton, according to the Duke of Wellington. And he should know. We think it's nice to call someone a sport and don't like foul play. In fact the word 'sportsman' is untranslatable into any language, just as 'gentleman' and 'fair play' are, and other countries use these terms in the original.

Without doubt it is cricket that has penetrated furthest into the national psyche. We talk about doing something off our own bat or something that's not cricket, being stumped, batting on a sticky wicket, being caught out and keeping a straight bat, etc. All very Wodehousian and quintessentially English. I once worked in a firm where the senior partner used to shout out 'end of play' when the office was closing and he used to refer to his partners as numbers 2 and 3 on the batting list. The ejaculation 'shiver my timbers' meaning 'I'll be damned', or as Tommy Handley might have put it, 'Knock me on my napper with a 9 inch nail' does not have a naval origin as I always thought: timbers was a slang word for wicket and the expression reflected the astonishment of a batsman at seeing his stumps and bails scattered on the ground.

The funny thing is that cricket isn't our national game. If there is one, it's soccer. Yet hardly anything has entered the language from soccer, except maybe to score an own goal. Other pastimes have influenced our ways of thinking and speaking. There are many terms from racing (champ at the bit, running neck and neck), boxing (take it on the chin, straight from the shoulder, out for the count), fishing (when you're really passionate about some interest, it is said you're hooked on it) and so on. Why is cricket so dominant? I think it's a class matter going back to Rudyard Kipling ('If') and Dr Thomas Arnold of Rugby more than a century ago, when gentlemen's games were fostered in the Victorian ethos of public schools and the boys were taught:

For when the One Great Scorer comes
To write against your name,
He marks — not that you won or lost —
But how you played the game.

Sadly, this concept of the game for the game's sake seems to have gone out of the window, replaced by depressing commercialism with sports grounds spattered by advertising of all manly occupations such as smoking, and promotions of a well-known male contraceptive. Even the Olympic Games have changed beyond all recognition. In 1936 Hitler was a bit of a joke as he stamped with fury when Jesse Owens, the black sprinter, won the 100 yards. Nowadays every competing nation is in it for the political glory of winning and you can't tell the women from the men, they are so full of steroids. Some of the athletes regard a gold medal not so much as an honourable award for excellence but as a lucrative springboard to promote running shoes and the like. The McEnroe syndrome has taken over.

This concentration on winning the game, whether it's soccer or even, yes, cricket, to the exclusion of all else and not just 'playing the game' has led to scenes which would have given Dr Arnold a nervous breakdown. I believe it's still bad form to take your shirt off at Lord's while watching a game on a hot summer day but when spectators both in the West Indies and here started to throw beer cans on the pitch I knew this was the beginning of the end. The rowdiness of the spectators has been encouraged by the excesses of the players which have permeated every game, including snooker — *pace* Hurricane Higgins.

Now what is your position if you are involved in violence or an accident at a sporting event, either as a player or spectator? In both cases account is always taken of the principle of *volenti non fit injuria,* which simply means a person cannot bring an action against anybody else if he has consented to the risk of injury or damage. For instance, if you are a boxer and lose a few teeth, or even your life, as happened not long ago to one of Barry McGuigan's opponents in the ring, you don't have a leg to stand on for any compensation you claim, as you go into it with your eyes open, even though you may come out with your eyes closed. This goes for the rough and tumble of most sports provided they are conducted according to the rules of the game. Violence outside the normally accepted rules can amount to assault. It can even be a criminal offence for causing g.b.h. (grievous bodily harm). David Bishop, the Welsh rugby player, was recently convicted of punching a player unconscious during a game between Pontypool and Newbridge. Following this disgraceful incident he was quite properly dropped from the team at the next international, and subsequently suspended by his club, Pontypool, for a year. He was sentenced to one month's imprisonment which was suspended for a year when he appealed. In another incident in 1985 a player had his ear bitten off in a 'friendly' match between two teams of (guess who?) policemen; the offender in this case was jailed for six months and his appeal was rejected.

However, it is usually only civil actions which are brought against the culprit for damages. In 1967, during a soccer match one player kicked another after a tackle, breaking his leg. The injured player was unable to play football again. He went to court and got £5,400 damages (Brookshaw v. Lewis).

Spectators, of course, suffer proportionately more injuries than players and there is a long line of cases showing that where an accident cannot reasonably (that's

the word again) be foreseen the injured party cannot claim any damages. Provided proper precautions are taken by the organizers you get nothing. If you take the risk of getting hit on the head by a football it's down to you. In a 1933 case (Hall v. Brooklands Auto Racing Club) several spectators were seriously injured when a racing car ploughed into their enclosure. It was held on appeal they had no case. All reasonable precautions had been taken and the spectators took upon themselves the risk of injury when they elected to attend the races. Dicing with death, as I believe it's called. A similar situation arose when a boy of six suffered serious injuries when he was hit by the puck at an ice-hockey match. He got nothing (Murray v. Harringay Arena 1951). This also goes for accidents at fairs, circuses and theatres. You pays your money and takes your choice. Yet a midget who suffered nervous shock at a circus after an elephant was frightened by a dog was awarded damages because it was shown that the elephant, although well-trained, ran amok and the circus proprietors were to blame.

What is the legal position if you are not even participating in the sporting event as a spectator when the accident occurs? For example, on a nice quiet Sunday afternoon you are peacefully walking your dog down the street minding your own business and the business of your dog with no cares in the world except maybe a slight feeling of guilt at having accepted that second helping of spotted dick an hour before, when you are suddenly laid flat by a cricket ball catching you between the eyes and knocking you for six. The ball has come from your local ground after a mighty drive by some budding Botham and has soared over the 17 foot fence surrounding the ground.

Where do you stand, as it were, after you have picked yourself up? Can you claim damages from the batsman or cricket club for your personal injuries? You can't, I am afraid. You are on a sticky wicket, as was the lady who caught a fourpenny one, a Miss Stone, who took the club to court. You see, the cricket club took all reasonable precautions and what happened could not reasonably have been foreseen. At least that's what the Judges said on appeal to the House of Lords in 1951.

Now I know why umpires in the old days used to wear lots of hats.

VAGRANCY ACT 1824 — ROGUES AND VAGABONDS AND INDECENT EXPOSURE

Under this Act you are a rogue and vagabond if you 'wilfully, openly, lewdly and obscenely expose your person with intent to insult any female'. 'Person' refers to 'penis' and not to other parts of the body, as was held in Evans v. Ewels (1972). I'm sorry to say you don't commit an offence under the Act by exposing any other part of your body with intent to insult a female. This probably accounts for the current spate of buttock baring, or 'mooning', as

I believe it's popularly called. This happens to be a traditional form of greeting in reverse in New Zealand apparently, where it goes under the name of 'whakapohane' which I would roughly translate as 'radical cheek'. Indeed, during the 1986 visit of Her Majesty the Queen to the Antipodes some disaffected Maoris prepared a '21-bum salute' for the Monarch. Kiri te Kanawa please note. Understandably, they are a bit behind down under.

In another case in 1972, Fulham half-back and Ireland international, James Dunne, appeared at Sunderland Magistrates Court charged with insulting behaviour. According to the prosecution, Dunne moved towards the crowd and without warning lowered the front of his shorts directly in view of the crowd. He then appeared to take out his private parts. It is not clear whether his private parts were fully exposed or whether they were still covered by the support straps he wore under his shorts. Dunne claimed he was only adjusting his jock strap. 'I was a bit uncomfortable at the time so I just pulled down my shorts a little bit and tucked my shirt inside. I never touched my private parts.' The Bench thought his story was a lot of Irish bull and touched his private pocket to the tune of £70. If he had not given a full frontal display but merely shown his backside I think he would have been acquitted (although in my view he was distinctly offside).

Talking of flashing, I can't forbear to tell the story about the flasher who was asked if he was going to retire. 'Well', he said, 'I was going to give it up but I thought I might just stick it out for another year or two.'

FORTUNE TELLERS, MEDIUMS AND HYPNOTISTS — MORE TALES OF THE UNEXPECTED

FORTUNE TELLERS
Do you ever read 'What the Stars Foretell' in the newspaper? I shouldn't be surprised if you do, however much you protest you don't believe what you are told. I always read mine. At least I look at the city pages, and the weather forecast, which almost amounts to the same thing

— and is about just as reliable. But did you know it is a criminal offence for someone to tell your fortune? Or to read your hands? People who do this are 'deemed Rogues and Vagabonds' by the Vagrancy Act 1824, which is still in force, and are liable to imprisonment for up to three months or a fine up to £400. You become a 'Rogue and Vagabond' by 'pretending or professing to tell fortunes, or using any subtle craft means or device, by palmistry or otherwise, to deceive and impose on any of Her Majesty's subjects'. The word 'device' does not include a conjuring trick. This welcome assurance was given in 1869 (Johnson v. Fenner). A Mr Fenner had stood on a chair with a crowd around him offering small paper parcels for a shilling, in which he had previously pretended to put several silver coins such as half-crowns and florins (quite a lot of money in 1869). Some of the parcels were purchased for that price and when opened contained only ha'pence and it was held that the hustler could not be convicted under the Act for using a subtle device 'by palmistry, or otherwise'. It seemed that the proper remedy was an indictment for obtaining money by false pretences. So if you are taken in by the three-card trick in Oxford Street you know what to do.

There have been some interesting cases on fortune telling. It is not necesary to prove that the defendant actually told the fortune of any individual; it is sufficient if he advertised an offer to do so (Penny v. Hanson 1887). Again your fortune teller may be quite sure in his own mind of the facts he is giving you and is thus not deceiving you but it is not necessary to prove any intention to deceive. Merely to tell fortunes is an offence in itself whatever the state of mind of the fortune teller (Stonehouse v. Masson 1921).

Now don't start getting on to the police to prosecute the *News of the World* for telling you, a Pisces or Gemini or whatever your sign, that you were going to meet the man of your dreams who didn't materialize. A case on these grounds (Barbanell v. Naylor 1936) was heard by three Judges, one of whom was the Lord Chief Justice, Lord Hewart, and another who in later years held the post,

Lord Goddard. The Bench said the newspaper article was addressed to the public generally and forecast the future of all persons born on a certain day. It didn't purport to tell the fortune of an individual and was thus not caught by the Act. A very tolerant view of the Zodiac, I would have thought. Hardly an outcome to be predicted, even by the writer of the article. Yet who knows? Perhaps Lord Goddard had read that he was ordained for higher things in the same article and to become Lord Chief Justice. As for Lord Hewart, he was, in the words of Lord Devlin, 'a horror' while in office (The Judge, OUP 1979, p.24). The case gave him scope for his caprices, in fact a 'horrorscope'. Ouch.

But astrologers and palmists beware. If you claim to tell the fortune of an individual at a fair, the church garden party, or wherever — even at a party in your own home — you are in trouble, as the law stands. And it doesn't matter whether you are paid for it or not. Furthermore, if you carry on telling fortunes after your first conviction, you become in the eyes of the law 'an incorrigible rogue' and can be put in the slammer for 12 months. This should come as no surprise to palmists and astrologers, who should easily be able to tell by looking at their own mitts or horoscopes whether they are destined for the nick or not.

Which brings me to the scabrous tale of the man who suffered from haemorrhoids. A friend told him that he had suffered from the same complaint and had cured it by drinking lots and lots of tea. Which he did. At the end of the month he went to see his doctor, feeling somewhat better for the experience. He asked the doctor if he would examine him and the doctor asked him to bend down. As he did so he asked the doctor if he could see anything. The doctor looked closely, and after a minute replied: 'I see you're going to meet a tall dark stranger...'

MEDIUMS

I now come to the Fraudulent Mediums Act 1951. This was an act 'to repeal the Witchcraft Act 1735 and to make in substitution for certain provisions of the Vagrancy Act

1824 express provision for the punishment of persons who fraudulently purport to act as spiritualistic mediums or to exercise powers of telepathy, clairvoyance or other similar powers'. I imagine that in the 130 years between the Vagrancy Act and this Act, Parliament must have become increasingly nervous of the power of the mediums, not to say media (maybe they got it mixed up). Anybody guilty of an offence under this Fraudulent Mediums Act is in for two years behind bars, but no proceedings may be brought except with the consent of the Director of Public Prosecutions.

If I may use the phrase, I consider the Act a dead letter since it appears that no prosecution has ever been brought under it. Maybe this is because the Act specifically states that a person can only be charged who 'for reward, and not solely for the purpose of entertainment, with intent to deceive, purports to act as a spiritualistic medium or to exercise any powers of telepathy clairvoyance or any similar powers'. The operative words were 'with intent to deceive'. Who on earth (and I mean on earth) can prove this? Surely the court would have to rely on the testimony of *another* medium to provide evidence from the hereafter. And then a *third* to corroborate the second. And so on, and so on. The only case I can find pre-dates the Act. In R. v. Duncan (1944) a spiritualist medium was prosecuted under the Witchcraft Act of 1735 for claiming to communicate with the dead. In the course of a (spirited) defence Mrs Duncan offered to give the court a demonstration of her powers, which the Judge declined before giving the lady a demonstration of *his* powers.

Incidentally, my father, who as an undertaker was on intimate terms with death, used to casually let drop that he could talk to the dead. His friends, impressed, would ask what they said. 'Oh,' he would reply, 'they never talk back.'

HYPNOTISTS
Demonstrations of hypnotism as a public entertainment at theatres, etc, are strictly controlled by the Hypnotism Act

1952, or supposed to be. If you're going to hypnotize an audience you must get a licence first from the local council. Fair enough. But it is absolutely forbidden to hypnotize anyone under the age of 18 at a place of entertainment, with or without his or her consent. How many stage hypnotists check the birth certificates of their audience? I remember when exhibitions of hypnosis used to draw crowds of willing guinea pigs who would fall into a trance at the snap of the hypnotist's fingers. This seems to have gone out of fashion in recent years. I suppose now we have party political broadcasts on the telly there's no longer any need to traipse out to theatres to get mesmerized.

NOT PAYING YOUR BILL IN HOTELS AND RESTAURANTS

In R. v. Allen (Christopher), an Australian over here on holiday stayed at a hotel and left without paying the bill. When arrested and charged under Section 3 (1) of the Theft Act 1978 he said that he was expecting money from a business transaction which had not materialized and that he intended to pay the bill at the time. The trial court however relied on the wording of the Theft Act and the Judge directed the jury that the words 'with intent to avoid payment' should be taken into account, although his counsel strenuously argued that there was no permanent intention for the bill not to be paid. The case went to the Court of Appeal and then finally to the House of Lords when on 30 June 1985 Lord Hailsham, Lord Scarman, Lord Diplock, Lord Bridge and Lord Brightman, all Judges of the highest eminence, agreed that the first trial Judge was wrong and that if permanent intention not to pay cannot be proved there is no case to answer.

This ruling has very far-reaching implications for hotel owners and restaurant owners, because it seems that anybody can now fill himself up with lobster and Château Yquem and then do a bunk without paying the bill. For the malefactor it is a chance well worth taking since if he is caught he can always plead that it was his intention to pay anyway and that he was just temporarily out of funds, and, of course, if he is not caught he can work his way round all the London hotels starting at Claridges. Do not be surprised, therefore, if you see two or three waiters circling your table at the end of a convivial evening when you are presented with the bill. But remember. It's up to the jury to decide whether you were 'permanently' intending to evade payment.

A WORD IN YOUR EAR, NOT TO SAY ABSCESS

In 1938 a woman went to Whiteleys in Bayswater, a fashionable department store, and had her ears pierced by the store jeweller, and an abscess resulted in one of her ears. Could she claim from the jeweller or from the store? She couldn't. Ms Phillips, the lady pierced, lost her case, which was heard by Mr Justice Goddard who was later to become Lord Chief Justice and was thus no slouch. If you go to a jeweller and not a doctor for a minor operation of this kind you take the risk upon yourself. All you can expect is the ordinary care a jeweller with unsterilized instruments can provide, not the expert care you would expect from a surgeon, i.e. if you fly on a charter you can't complain if you don't get Concorde service, and this goes for a lot of negligence cases.

PAINTING THE TOWN (HOUSE) RED

You live in a Georgian terrace made up of 'listed' houses all painted in tasteful House and Garden shades, or they may all be white. Somebody moves in two doors down and decides to paint his house red or some other colour totally out of keeping with the colours of your house and your neighbours'. Can you do anything about it? Surprisingly, you can. He should have applied for planning permission, which, because his was a listed building, would almost certainly have been turned down.

The planning consent needed is for 'an alteration or extension' of the building and you can be prosecuted for carrying out such work under Section 55 of the Town and Country Planning Act 1971, but only if it's a listed building. A semi in Neasden is another matter. So is a holiday caravan in Yorkshire, as a local council there found to its cost in February 1986. They wanted the owner of the caravan, a Mr Robin Hood, no less, to repaint it in a dark colour to blend with the landscape. It was green and white, and this offended the council. But on appeal Mr Hood was allowed to keep it as it was. Not the first time a Mr R. Hood has had a brush with the authorities and come out of it with flying colours.

9

THE LEGAL PROFESSION

BARRISTERS AND SOLICITORS

Two small children were playing in a muddy field, a little boy and a little girl. One's father was a barrister, and the other's a solicitor. They got so muddy that they decided to take all their clothes off and wipe themselves down. When the little girl had taken all her clothes off the little boy said to her 'Gosh, I didn't know there was all that much difference between barristers and solicitors'.

It is not a *petite différence*. The umbrella term for both barristers and solicitors is 'lawyers' and if you say that someone is a lawyer he can be either a barrister or a solicitor, but not both as this country remains one of the few places where the professions are still quite separate. Strange to say, I believe they have more in common with each other than not. For instance, anybody who has seen a solicitor or barrister will know that they both share a predilection for demonstrating that 2 and 2 make 5. This is not as difficult as it looks, as this algebraic equation reveals:

$$\text{Let } X = Y$$
$$\text{then } X^2 = Y^2$$
$$\text{and } X^2 - XY = X^2 - Y^2$$
$$\therefore X(X-Y) = (X-Y)(X+Y)$$
$$\text{Dividing out the common factor } (X-Y)$$
$$\text{we have } X = X+Y$$
$$\therefore X = 2X$$
$$\therefore 1 = 2$$

But as a cynic has said '*You* must be frank and explicit with your lawyer ... it is his business to confuse the issue afterwards'.

One strange thing about barristers though is that *they don't shake hands with each other*. Perfectly true. Nobody can tell me why. Whether it's because they feel they may lose a few fingers in the process or may catch something I just can't say. But there you are.

There are about 45,000 solicitors in the country as against 5,000 barristers. Solicitors, not entirely unreasonably, have a bit of a chip on their shoulder about barristers, who enjoy amenities and privileges and curiously a higher social and (in the eyes of the layman) professional status, all denied to solicitors. And they both have a chip about not being able to put letters of distinction after their names, like doctors and dentists, etc. (except for QCs). Here are a few more peculiarities of the Bar.

JUDGES
If you want to become a Judge you must be a barrister or a solicitor. However, the Bench, with few exceptions, is appointed entirely from barristers, and if you want to be a High Court Judge you must be a barrister.

NEGLIGENCE
While you can quite properly sue a solicitor — as you can a member of any other profession — for negligence, i.e. for bungling your case, barristers are totally immune from suits for negligence arising out of court proceedings. This is a highly prized privilege. Two contributors to Counsel, the Bar's trade journal, writing in 1986 on professional indemnity insurance cover (which all barristers must have for work out of court) says 'there is insufficient appreciation in the market of the specially favourable position of the Bar as a profession (no liability for court work, *difficulties in proving damage, etc*). The Bar has suffered by association in underwriters' minds ... with other professional groups.' You can sue them if they give you what turns out to be incorrect advice in the form of a Counsel's Opinion, as it's called, but if they misrepresent your case in court and deal with it so badly that you lose it you can't do much about it, I am afraid. This is because it is the unanimous view of the judiciary (that is, all the Judges) that it would be against 'public policy' for you to

The Legal Profession

do so. These are magic words always invoked when it is felt the interests of the State or the community are at risk. All very high-minded you may think: but for a Judge to declare something is contrary to public policy simply means that he thinks it wrong to allow it. In fairness to the Bench it must be said that the rather shadowy concept of public policy has been a source of debate, if not downright ridicule, over the ages. In a celebrated case in 1824 (Richardson v. Mellish) a Judge said 'I, for one, protest against arguing too strongly upon public policy — it is a very unruly horse, and when once you get astride it you never know where it will carry you'. In 1938 (Fender v. St John-Mildmay) Lord Atkin said in the House of Lords 'It is the province of the Judge to expound the law only ... not to speculate upon what is the best, in his opinion, for the advantage of the community'.

Nonetheless most Judges are promoted barristers, and blood is thicker than water.

FEES
What is more, if a barrister accepts a brief and receives payment of his fees but for some reason does not attend at the trial you can't do anything about it at all. You can't get your money back and you can't claim damages from him for not showing up. These were the regrettable facts in Turner v. Philipps (1792) and Robertson v. Macdonogh (1880), and both precedents still stand. On the other hand a barrister cannot sue for *his* fees — if the client doesn't pay up that is tough for the barrister.

Be it noted that if you think a solicitor has overcharged you, you can always apply to the Law Society for what is called a Remuneration Certificate to establish that his charges were indeed fair and reasonable and if they weren't you can get some of your money back, if not all of it. The Bar has no similar system. I think this is a bit hard on the lay client, particularly as it is probably a one-off experience for him. He has no idea what is going on and leaves things in the hands of his solicitor who won't shop around as much as *he* would to get the best deal. Lord Templeman, a senior Judge, is quite acerbic about barristers' charges. 'I think the Bar Council ought to get out of its ivory tower, and in the same way as you can go to the Law Society to find if a solicitor is charging too much, I don't see why the Bar Council shouldn't be asked to do the same function for barristers.'

At the top end fees are enormous: at the bottom end, paltry. But very often you pay the master's fees for work done by the servant. This is the principal of 'devilling', a sort of sub-contracting. It is something like 'ghosting'. The dictionary definition of 'devilling' is 'doing hackwork especially for a lawyer or author; performing arduous tasks often without pay or recognition of one's services'. A barrister will frequently delegate a lot of the donkey work to a poorly paid junior barrister, or even a pupil, who will draft a document or write an opinion (the Bar Council now accept that a 50-50 split in the fees is a fair deal for the devil). But the work goes out in the name of the principal who, of course, vets the finished job — or should do — before it goes out and gets paid for it at the full rate.

Another profitable quirk of the system arises when a case is settled out of court. By far the majority of cases are settled in this way, since one of the litigants will come to his senses sooner or later before the trial and cave in. Whether a settlement is made at the door of the court or the day after the barrister gets his brief, he is still entitled to the original fee negotiated — in full. It is otherwise with solicitors who only charge for work actually done: if you see a solicitor one day and instruct him on a lengthy and complicated matter then change your mind the next day, he will only charge you for the one consultation. To be sure, barristers are not allowed to sue solicitors (or the lay client) for unpaid fees, but the word soon gets around if the solicitor doesn't pay a barrister and he will have to put the fees up front before another barrister will do work for him.

Some readers may think it a good idea for lawyers to be paid on results, as is very often the case in America, that is on a 'contingency' basis — you pay nothing if you get nothing. There are arguments for and against, though the prime argument against is that anyone with a weak case will not be able to get proper representation — when they may be the very people who most need decent counsel.

NO SHOPPING AROUND FOR QUOTES
Nowadays you can ring round and get estimates and quotations from solicitors for any work you want to give them, although the 'Solicitors Accounts Rules' expressly provide that it is only in rare cases that it is proper for a solicitor to give a firm quotation. However solicitors often break this rule, but mainly for so-called non-contentious matters such as wills and conveyances. Not so with barristers. There is a very quaint system whereby it is not etiquette for a barrister to discuss his fee with a solicitor (let alone with the lay client, i.e. you). A solicitor will deal with a barrister's clerk, and if you think the bar is a closed shop you want to look at how clerks operate. Their jobs are so profitable that they are handed down from father to son. The clerk negotiates the fee with the solicitor and takes a cut of about 10 per cent of the barrister's fee. Human nature being what it is, clerks are a bit like insurance brokers, who mainly make their living out of commission on the policies they sell. The bigger the insurance, the more they make. No comment. (But comment can be found in 'The Svengalis of the law', page 155).

ONLY A BARRISTER CAN REPRESENT YOU IN HIGHER COURTS
Apart from county courts and inferior courts such as magistrates courts, only barristers have a right of audience. This means that solicitors cannot represent a client in the High Court or Court of Appeal or House of Lords.

BUT A BARRISTER WON'T SEE YOU ON YOUR OWN
A barrister mustn't visit a solicitor in his office. Mahomet must go to the mountain. Furthermore, if a barrister is going to represent you in court or even if you want his advice on some matter as a layman you must always be chaperoned by a solicitor. His professional rules do not

allow him to see you alone — so you have to pay two sets of fees. In fact, if you brief a silk, which means a Queen's Counsel, he will not normally appear without a junior. So you can end up paying *three* sets of fees (I think this was the start of over-manning in this country). This is all very well if you want judgement at all costs and the money is coming out of your own pocket but it must be remembered that over 40 per cent of barristers' fees come from legal aid work, so we are *all* affected at the end of the day since money to pay all these fees comes out of the public purse.

LIMITS ON LAW CENTRES

The amount of free legal advice given by newspapers and other forms of the media to people who write or phone in shows that there is a tremendous need for it by people who can't afford to see a lawyer. There are many barristers who, to their credit, give their services at law centres free of charge, but the Bar Council places very strict limits on what they may do. They may not:

a)   appear as an advocate in courts in the course of their work at the centre

b)   sue out any writ or process

c)   instruct Counsel

d)   carry out conveyancing work.

This emasculation really takes the ground away from under the feet of such centres, many of which are closing down anyway due to government cut-backs. This is a sad reflection on our caring society, and even Edward Heath, not exactly a militant leftwinger, as long ago as 1967 pinpointed 'the comparative failure of the legal advice mechanism' which he saw as 'a rather half-hearted solution to the real problem of poverty, of ignorance, of timidity in the face of the law', and a case of 'one law for the rich and one for the poor'.

NO PARTNERSHIPS

Barristers cannot form partnerships with other barristers. They are self-employed, as distinct from solicitors who can and do blame their partners if things go wrong.

THE CONSERVATISM OF THE BAR

The bar is restrictive, as I have shown, in its professional practices and it is ultra-conservative in others. Most barristers work in a tiny area of London in one of the four Inns of Court. The Inns have great power. They are a mixture of college, selection board, disciplinary body and club. They are ruled by Benchers who are a group of senior lawyers who elect themselves and who are curiously exempted from publishing accounts.

THE BAR'S RETICENCE

On top of all this, the Bar is very defensive. The top 'Barman' is Lord Hailsham, the Lord Chancellor. He appoints Judges and has the last say. He also has a way with words. In a lengthy interview that he gave in *The Sunday Times* (25 August 1985) he confided to John Mortimer (and about four million readers) that when he sits on the Woolsack in the House of Lords he amuses himself by saying 'bollocks' to the bishops. Under his

breath, of course, since I have never seen this reported in Hansard. Very amusing. I don't know how he would take it if the bishops riposted by chanting in unison 'up yours'. Under their breath, of course. At least this would sound wittier than the usual run of parliamentary exchanges. However, despite his gifts of expression, he rarely appears on television or speaks on the radio. When invited to participate in a recent radio programme (*Pillars of Society*) on which other eminent jurists appeared, he not only had nothing to say but tried to make sure that no other Judges spoke on the programme.

This being said, the Bar is currently undergoing considerable self-flagellation. There are action groups and ginger groups, and in an unprecedented move barristers, who have complained that they are so grossly underpaid that some of them have to work in Chinese restaurants, took the Lord Chancellor to court over the way he has ridden roughshod over their claims for more money. The action was adjourned once it became obvious that the Lord Chancellor was on to a hiding to nothing — he agreed to negotiate with the Bar on fees. After pursuing a claim for a 30-40 per cent rise, the Bar has now meekly accepted 10 per cent.

THEIR COSTUME
Like Judges, barristers have a ritualistic get-up as far as their dress is concerned. They wear wigs and wing collars, gowns and tabs, and women barristers have to dress up to look as much like men as possible. It has solemnly been said that this is necessary to set them apart from the jeans and trainer crowd, although a lot of barristers don't share this view and feel it only frightens and humiliates witnesses whom they cross-examine.

THEIR EFFICIENCY
How efficient are barristers? Well, for a start, despite their fancy dress and quaint customs and restrictive practices they are human and have the same frailties as you or I. There are probably as many adulterers and homosexuals

and even criminals among them as in any cross-section of the community. No so long ago a certain barrister forged a will and blackmailed a former girl friend by threatening to publish pornographic photographs he had taken of her. He did a bunk and has never been heard of again. But of course, the vast majority are law-abiding and maintain the highest professional and personal standards.

While not giving ground on the immunity of barristers from claims for negligence in court, the Bar Council recognized that barristers can slip up in giving advice or Counsel's Opinions, and makes it a rule that *all* barristers must take up professional indemnity insurance cover (like solicitors) for at least £250,000. To my simple mind it seems that the likelihood of negligence in court is just as great as out of court and I would like to see this privilege abolished. No other profession is so feather-bedded.

Just as medical students are taught that half the patients they see they won't be able to cure while the other half will get better anyway, so it has been said of lawsuits that 'of every hundred cases, ninety win themselves, three are won by advocacy and seven are lost by advocacy'. On the other hand it has been said 'A jury consists of twelve persons to decide who has the better lawyer' (Robert Frost).

It seems that as with most things in life you get what you pay for. Litigation is a very expensive pastime. Whenever a client comes to me wanting to 'sue the bastards' — and this is by no means an infrequent occurrence — I try and deflect him from going to court. We are impressed to be told proudly that the courts of England are open to all citizens, but then, so are the doors of the Ritz Hotel. If you want lobster and champagne you have to pay for it. If you are willing to make do with hamburgers you go to a burger bar.

THE SVENGALIS OF THE LAW

You are a barrister. Whom do you hold most dear? Who is the most important person in your life? The Lord Chancellor? Your head of chambers? The solicitor who sends you briefs? Patric Walker, the astrologer? Your wife? Your mistress? Your mother? No, none of these. It is your clerk. Barristers' clerks have an authority and power out of all proportion to their ostensibly menial position and qualifications. They are the 'fixers' of the profession, mostly self-employed, and a very select body. In all they only number about 300, of whom 200 are in London. They are rarely salaried and earn their living by taking a 'cut' of the fees they negotiate for the barristers in their charge — usually about 10 per cent (briefs of £250,000, while scarce, are not exceptional). A senior Judge, Vice-Chancellor Megarry, has described the clerk as 'a complicated cross between a theatrical agent, a business manager, an accountant, and a trainer'. To which I would add 'protector and taskmaster'.

Charles Lamb's father was a clerk. To his principal 'he was at once his clerk, his good servant, dresser, his friend, his guide, stop-watch, auditor, treasurer. He did nothing without consulting him, or failed in anything without expecting and fearing his admonishing.' Still very true of many barrister-clerk relationships today.

The clerk thus seems to be a paragon of all the virtues. Don't be misled. The Times thought they were quite disorganized. In a leader in 1959 they came out with a blockbuster: 'The office inefficiency of many barristers' chambers is a disgrace to a profession. This is because they are not run by barristers, but by their clerks, who are wholly untrained in business methods.'

Since then things have improved a bit, but not a lot. In 1970 a Methods Manual was brought out for their guidance, but J. A. Flood, who conducted a detailed study of clerks in 1983 (Barristers Clerks, the Law's Middlemen, Manchester University Press 1983) has said that on his visits to their offices 'I found little trace of the manual; if there was one, it was usually ... in the bottom of a drawer under a pile of papers. Some clerks had never seen it. They would look at my copy, only to hand it back with a derisory comment.' Their secrecy regarding their earnings speaks for itself. As one clerk put it, 'the barrister earns 90 per cent of the clerk's fee.' But they don't like talking about it: only half of them replied to an earnings questionnaire for the Royal Commission on Legal Services in 1979.

What is more, while the officer-sergeant major relationship of barristers and solicitors has been thought to verge on the sado-masochistic (Michael Zander, *Lawyers and the Public Interest,* Weidenfeld and Nicolson 1968) this is nothing compared to that between barrister and clerk. In fact, the functions of a clerk bear a distinct similarity to those of a madam in a brothel who enjoys with her working sisters power without responsibility ('the prerogative of the harlot through the ages'), but it must be said that I am not well up on brothels and am open to correction by more experienced readers. I make no apologies, however, for drawing the parallel. Baudelaire wrote (*Intimate Journals,* 1887): 'There is no exalted pleasure that cannot be related to prostitution.' I don't know how many barristers regard their calling as an exalted pleasure but the simile still stands.

Basically, it is the clerk's job to fix a barrister's fee with the solicitor, from which, as I have said, he takes a commission of up to 10 per cent and makes sure it is paid, and — what is even more important — to obtain and dish out work to the barristers in his chambers. This is more of an art than you might think and many successful barristers owe their progress to a competent clerk, or to be more accurate, to their *relationship* with a competent clerk. No wonder they are beholden to him, as the following quotation illustrates even more forcefully: 'There are still a few members of the Bar who would not take a day off without their clerk's approval ... and who can almost be regarded as their clerk's man rather than their own.' No, not a dig from the *Solicitors Journal* but a statement in 1979 to the Royal Commission on Legal Services by — the Senate of the Bar Council.

Are you beginning to see the resemblance to the manageress of a bordello? She can make or mar the careers of her charges; she it is who parades them to her clients while trying to assess the latters' proclivities. She

Sir Willoughby Dimley

Presen

negotiates a price and then collects it, paying part over to the chosen ladies of the house. No wonder they toe the line. But the analogy stops there. Madams are usually superannuated cocottes of very wide experience. Their qualifications have been gained on the job, as it were, and clerks need no such qualifications to enter the field. All they need is an English O level — not a very exacting requirement.

The Bar Council does not see the system as in any way archaic (no other country has it, by the way) nor as disturbing for the public or their own members. They do not regard it as strange that a clerk's standard of living should depend on the commission he earns from his principal's fees. Surely, unless he is less than human he will try and make these as high as possible. Or that a barrister's career, certainly in its early stages, should be in the hands of his clerk. A bit like the tail wagging the dog. But this is all OK by the Bar Council — even though it was openly conceded in evidence to the Royal Commission that some clerks sold barristers short 'because of personal antipathy or some prejudice relating to class, race or colour'. The oddest thing though, is that most barristers seem happy to put up with the system.

But not all is sweetness and light. In 1985 a barrister himself stood trial at the Old Bailey on two charges of assaulting his senior clerk in a pub near the Law Courts, causing him actual bodily harm. I wonder why.

SOLICITORS' SINS OF COMMISSION

Sometimes a solicitor encourages you to take out an insurance policy, or invest some money in a building society, or he may act for you on a purchase of stocks and shares (that is quite common when a solicitor handles family trusts, for example). In such cases the solicitor may earn commission from the insurance company, which on the purchase of a life policy can be very substantial, sometimes the whole of the first year's premium, and likewise in the case of building societies (most building societies pay for the introduction of investments, usually about 1 per cent of the amount invested although some smaller building societies pay quite a bit more). This commission, however, does not in reality belong to the solicitor. It belongs to the *client*, and the solicitor can only retain it on the express authority of the client. In other words he should automatically pass it to you unless you tell him he can keep it. The rules of the Law Society are quite clear. You will find them on page 24 of the solicitors' professional book of rules under the heading *Secret Profits*. However, this appears to be a rule more honoured in the breach than in the observance. I am not suggesting for one moment that solicitors deliberately deceive their clients and pocket the money: I feel that most solicitors simply do not know this rule, but of course they should. In 1920 in the case of Jordy v. Vanderpump it was ruled 'the onus is on a solicitor to show ... that his client knew of and consented to his receiving and retaining commission paid to him as agent by an insurance company in respect of ... a policy effected on the life of his client'.

Readers may recall the mammoth British Telecom share issue in December 1984. Any solicitor who as an intermediary sent in a share application for his client earned 1¼ per cent commission on the total consideration involved. So that if, say, you sent in an application through him for 800 shares and put down £400 which was the first instalment, he eventually earned not 1¼ per cent of £400 but 1¼ per cent of £1,040, the total value of the shares, when they had been fully paid, i.e. £13. For the solicitor this was virtually a rubber-stamping operation. I regarded the payment of this commission as quite unjustified and almost immoral, and asked my clients if they would authorize me to send all the commission or at least part of it to Oxfam for Ethiopia Relief.

Next time you buy an insurance policy or whatever through your solicitor, ask him to be good enough to account to you for any commission he receives.

SOLICITOR'S MISTAKES — WHO PAYS?
Say your father or mother makes a will and leaves you

£5,000 but the solicitor who draws up the will omits to put this legacy in the document and nobody notices. Your parent dies and you look forward to receiving £5,000 which you had been expecting for many years as your inheritance. How do you stand? Well, it certainly appears that the solicitor will be liable in negligence to you and will have to cough up the £5,000 from his own pocket. He was instructed to carry out a transaction to confer benefit on you, an identified third person, and he therefore owes a duty to you to use proper care in carrying out the instructions. He must make good any loss you suffer.

This was the reasoning in Ross v. Caunters (1980), when solicitors instructed by the testator, that is the person who makes the will, allowed the spouse of a beneficiary to witness the will. As I have said (page 105), if a will is witnessed by a beneficiary, or the spouse of a beneficiary, the beneficiary loses all benefit under the will. In this particular case, since the husband of the beneficiary who was entitled to the residue of all the estate witnessed the will, his wife lost all the benefit. He claimed for damages. The solicitors admitted negligence but argued that a duty of care was owed only to the testator. This was a leading case actually heard by a very senior Judge, so his decision is unlikely to be overruled. The Judge said that the solicitors did indeed owe the beneficiary a duty of care since it was within the solicitors' direct contemplation that the beneficiary would suffer by their failure to carry out the testator's instructions. This case has very important implications therefore for any transaction where a third party suffers loss following a solicitor's carelessness in acting for another party. And quite right too.

JUDGES

The Law is the true embodiment
Of everything that's excellent.
It has no kind of fault or flaw
And I, my Lords, embody the Law
W.S. Gilbert, *Iolanthe*

Judges are human beings. They have families of
their own, familes have troubles. Judges have
friends who get into trouble. Judges have bills
to pay, they have arrangements to make. They
are not set apart, they are not cushioned. They
are not surrounded by menials. They have to lead
pretty normal lives off the Bench.

Lord Edmund-Davies, former Lord of Appeal in Ordinary

Some Judges are more human than others though. Sir
Francis Bacon (who wrote the *Essays* and was Queen
Elizabeth I's Lord Chancellor), found himself in the Tower
accused of taking £100,000 in bribes (a colossal sum in
1621), and although quickly released on payment of a fine
of £40,000 he was never given a full pardon. Lord Reading
as Attorney-General speculated in Marconi shares in 1913,
causing heads to shake and leading to a parliamentary
debate on his probity. This did not stop him becoming Lord
Chief Justice a few months later, a gift from King George
V for services rendered.

In recent years we have seen a top Judge in Australia
up for corruption. In Israel the Deputy Judge at the
Eichmann trial was found later to have no formal legal
qualifications and was sacked. At home we've had the
spectacle in 1985 of a deputy High Court Judge unseated
after he bounced a cheque of £1,000 in payment of a fine
for a VAT offence. (He admitted in court having four
previous convictions for a similar offence.) Another deputy
Judge was one of the first people to be prosecuted for kerb
crawling, although his conviction was quashed on appeal.
Even Lord Denning has had a brush with his local town
planning office for an infringement of planning law when
he built a brick wall at his home without the proper
consents.

These transgressors are of course the mavericks of the
Bench, who in general maintain its great tradition of
exemplary rectitude and incorruptibility. That being said,
Judges tend to lead their own lives and display great
individuality. Eyebrows were raised in 1970 when Sir

Henry Fisher, a respected High Court Judge, and the son of a former Archbishop of Canterbury, resigned from the Bench to become director of a merchant bank ('unprecedented and unacceptable', said Viscount Dilhorne, a former Lord Chancellor). Another, Mr Christmas Humphries, was a lifelong Buddhist. Lord Devlin has recently taken the lid off what happened in a sensational case he tried in 1956, that of John Bodkin Adams, accused of poisoning one of his patients and by implication several others (*Easing the Passing*, Bodley Head 1985). In this extraordinary instance the Judge (Lord Devlin) wrote a book about a case over which he presided, and in doing so made some very personal and quite scathing findings about the witnesses and counsel.

Some judgements have outraged public opinion, mostly for their leniency. Rapists have been virtually patted on the head and told not to do it again, and a raped woman has been told she was guilty of 'contributory negligence'. Such perversity has led the present Lord Chief Justice, Lord Lane, to lay down new guidelines for stiffer sentencing.

There have been many other bizarre pronouncements. In 1985 Judge Richard Pearce, hearing the evidence of a drug pusher to whom he gave a suspended sentence, said '4 or 5 happy, well-adjusted undergraduates can take LSD sitting around the fire listening to nice music without there being too much risk'.

How do you become a Judge? In most other countries in the West you train for it: it's a separate profession. After your law studies you can opt to take up judging as a career and work your way up the ladder. In those countries there are thousands of Judges against under 500 here. In the USA it is very often a political office and a reward for supporting the party elected to power. In this country you become a High Court Judge on invitation by the Lord Chancellor, and the only formal qualification you must have is to be a barrister of ten years' standing. The rest depends on the dossier kept on you by the Lord Chancellor's Department which is referred to as the 'yellow sheets'. On these are noted as much as can be gleaned of your professional, social and private life. By and large the system seems to work, although the disparity in sentencing between one Judge and another is disturbing. It has been said that Judges 'rely on a combination of 90 per cent inspiration and 10 per cent desperation' when deciding on a sentence. Why not a special panel for sentencing serious offenders?

Finally, a few judicial peculiarities.

— Working Hours.   High Court Judges normally sit from 10.30 a.m. to 4.30 p.m. with an hour's break for lunch, but of course they have to read the papers in every case, write judgements and do various administrative work.

— Fringe benefits.   In a maiden assize, that is one in which nobody is to be brought to trial, the Judge used to be presented with a pair of white gloves. Even today, senior Judges are sometimes given a posy or nosegay whose original intention was to ward off the stench of jail-fever. When Judges go on circuit they can take with them their own cook in case a disgruntled offender tries to poison them, a butler to keep their sherry uncontaminated, a clerk who helps them on with their robes, and a marshal to protect them from highwaymen. Very often they draw an allowance in lieu. Why can't they stay at the local Holiday Inn or wherever and rely on the boys in blue for protection? Some good housekeeping called for?

— Pay and Pension.   The full pension of a Judge is two-thirds his final year's salary if married, half if not, index-linked in either case. A High Court Judge earns about £60,000 a year.

— Dismissal.   High Court Judges can only be removed from office at the request of both Houses of Parliament, and then only on the ground of moral delinquency or incapacitating illness, but no Judge has been unseated in this way since 1700. If it is thought that a Judge shouldn't carry on any more, the etiquette is that he will resign. In 1891 one who went gaga resigned after a leader in The Times pointed the way. Some years before, efforts had been made to remove from office a Plymouth magistrate, a Mr James Bagg, a previous Mayor of the city, for insulting behaviour towards his successor, a Thomas Fowens. Mr

Bagg had turned his backside to Mr Fowens and invited him to kiss it. The Court held that there were no grounds for dismissing Mr Bagg, who carried on with his judicial duties. But that was in 1615: if a magistrate did the same today I think it would be regarded as a bare-faced breach of his authority and he would have to back down.

— Should a Judge pay your costs if he gives a decision which is wrong in law?   A High Court Judge is not liable to pay the costs of an appeal against his decisions, but a County Court Judge or magistrate might have to do so, although there are few recorded cases. Also, isn't it rather unfair that if your case goes to the Court of Appeal and then on to the House of Lords and at the end of the day a majority of Judges have been on your side, you should get no help with your enormous costs? This actually happened in an action between a Mr Vergottis and a certain Mr Onassis and Madame Callas. Mr Vergottis lost the case in the House of Lords by a majority of three to two, that is two Judges there thought he was correct. In the Court of Appeal three Judges had ruled in his favour. In all, five superior court Judges thought he was right and only four didn't.

Obviously, we can't expect the Judges to cough up money out of their own pockets to an aggrieved litigant, otherwise the whole Bench would be evacuated overnight. Shouldn't the State intervene in borderline decisions such as these and help out the loser with his costs?

— Clothing conventions.   Judges expect witnesses and certainly barristers to appear in court 'properly dressed'. If a barrister doesn't wear a waistcoat the Judge won't 'see' him, and a woman in trousers is a Judge's *bête noire*. The strange thing is that they see nothing peculiar about their own fancy dress. In common with peers, bishops and ambassadors, they all dress up as women when they want to put on the Ritz and go in for long robes or skirts, and black drawers and hose with buckled shoes. The introduction of tights for ladies brought welcome relief to many snappy dressers who beforehand had to rely on suspender belts to keep their stockings up. True. The story

is told of the late lamented Lord George-Brown who, at a diplomatic function when the orchestra struck up, felt that as the senior British minister present he should start the dancing. He spied a likely prey and said 'Madam, will you do me the honour of this waltz?' 'Certainly not', was the reply. 'For three reasons. First, you're drunk. Second, this is not a waltz but the Venezuelan national anthem. Third, I am the Papal Nuncio.'

— Pubs.   These are pleasures a Judge has to forsake when elevated to the Bench. It is not a rule of law but extremely inadvisable for Judges to pop in for a quick one, much as this may be to their taste, and though Lord Scarman strolled round Brixton recently chatting to all and sundry he was never seen with a pint in his hand. This is understandable, as a Judge could easily find himself having a natter at the bar with someone up before him the next day, and his conduct could be misinterpreted.

A story went round some years ago of the Archbishop of Canterbury (it has also been told of a Judge) who on arriving by transatlantic liner in New York was asked by a reporter if he intended to visit any striptease clubs in Brooklyn. He asked in return whether there were indeed any such clubs in Brooklyn. The next day the headlines splashed across the front page read 'Archbishop asks on arrival if there are any striptease clubs in Brooklyn'.

SOME COMPLAINTS ABOUT THE WORKINGS OF THE COURTS

I am not happy about what goes on in our courts. Here are a few of my gripes.

OATHS

A film star once described himself in the witness box as 'the greatest living actor'. 'How can you say that?' interrupted the Judge. 'Well, my Lord, you must understand I am on oath.' Not quite on a par with Oscar Wilde, who, when asked by a customs man on arriving back in the country if he had anything to declare, replied 'Only my genius'. But still pretty good — about seven on the Richter scale.

Why do witnesses or signatories of affidavits have to take any form of oath at all? Isn't this a little *passé* nowadays? Years ago it might have put the fear of God into witnesses and propelled them towards the path of righteousness. Indeed, the *Oxford Companion to Law* even now solemnly defines the oath as 'an assertion or promise made in the belief that supernatural retribution will fall on the taker if he violates what he swears to do'. But I don't think this puts the likes of Arthur Daley off very much, do you?

In *Halsbury's Laws* there are no less than 77 separate commentaries on oaths following on the Oaths Act of 1961

and 1978 in which there are special provisions for non-Christians: Jewish witnesses keep their heads covered and swear on the Old Testament, Chinese break saucers and atheists or agnostics may 'affirm', i.e. make a solemn declaration, and children under 14 'promise' but do not 'swear' (more of this under 'Children in court' on page 171). So you see it's exercised the minds of our law-makers quite a bit. But why bother? The form of the oath is as follows: 'I swear by Almighty God that the evidence I shall give shall be the truth, the whole truth and nothing but the truth' (the words 'so help me God', which used to follow, are no longer used). While this is a consummation devoutly to be wished, it's not very worldly.

The words of the oath are pretty meaningless anyway. What is 'the whole truth'? This often includes hearsay, that is, what you have heard from other people in conversation with them. It would be quite natural for a witness of an accident to describe it to his wife immediately afterwards — this would be part of 'the whole truth' — but no Judge would let him talk about it in the witness box. Again, he may have difficulty months or even years later at the trial to remember exactly what happened. But a person who gives his honest, albeit inaccurate, recollection of events cannot be guilty of perjury: this offence is committed only in the *deliberate* telling of falsehood. Incidentally, you can't get off a charge of perjury by saying afterwards that you were an atheist and not bound by the oath if you took the oath in a form accepted by you without objection (Perjury Act 1911 Section 15(1)). What is more, many Christians, particularly Quakers, see the taking of oaths as contrary to the teaching of Christ and setting up a double standard of truthfulness. They believe sincerity and truth should be practised in all dealings of life. I agree. It is open to all witnesses to elect to 'affirm' — i.e. to say 'I do solemnly, sincerely, and truly declare and affirm that the evidence ...' etc, but why not just tell *all* witnesses that they must give their evidence to the best of their honest belief and if it's found they have been telling lies they will end up in clink? Mind you, I'm not suggesting that solicitors should be stopped from administering the oath when you swear an affidavit. This is an important source of income to us (and so it should be, at three quid a time).

ARE YOU SITTING COMFORTABLY? STAND YOUR GROUND

I have always been bemused by the terminology relating to sitting, standing and running. In this country if you want to be an MP you stand for Parliament, and in America you run for office; you won't stand for something but might take it sitting down and when a trial is taking place the court is said to be sitting. We all know what a sit-down is, but can you have a stand-down? You can. When you leave the witness box you are said to stand down. A divorce lawyer, acting for the husband on a petition for nullity on the grounds of non-consummation, advised him against defending it with the words 'I don't really think it'll stand up in court'. Devotees of American television courtroom dramas will know that witnesses sit at the (witness) stand while the attorneys in best *Dynasty* fashion stride backwards and forwards putting their arguments.

In November 1985 a Mr Tegenrasing went to the Court of Appeal because a lower court, the Cambridge County Court, refused to hear his evidence while he remained seated in the witness box. The appeal court decided, however, that Mr Tegenrasing had no business wanting to give his evidence sitting down and found against him. Mr T. should have counted his blessings. The Judge in Cambridge did not take him into custody forthwith for his contrariness, or make an order committing him to prison for 'a specified period not exceeding one month' as he might well have done under Section 118(1) of the County Courts Act 1984. I think that would have made Mr Tegenrasing sit up, if not stand up. Mr T.'s behaviour was not as unbecoming as that of a dissatisfied plaintiff, a Mr Gohoho, who as *The Times* reported in 1964 took off all his clothes except for his shirt and lay down on a bench in the Court of Appeal after a disagreeable judgement against him. He got seven days for that.

SLEEPING ON THE JOB
It is not unknown for some Judges to be afflicted with deafness, or at least be hard of hearing and, yes, for a Judge to fall asleep during the trial. In 1972 two men accused of murder appealed against their conviction on what the Lord Chief Justice called 'the somewhat unusual ground that the Judge, at material times, either was asleep or appeared to be asleep'; and each contended that, on that ground, justice was not seen to be done and that the proper course was to order a new trial on the fresh evidence of the Judge's conduct. There seemed to be ample evidence that the trial court Judge, Mr Justice Crichton, had indeed nodded off, but the Court of Appeal decided that this couldn't have been the case because his notes showed that he had missed nothing ...

In another case in 1981 a man on a charge of careless driving complained that the chairperson was asleep during the hearing. The lady in question had said that it was her custom to close her eyes and look down. But was she taking her cue from the lady on the top of the dome of the Old Bailey, the statue of Justice, who is blindfolded? In any event the appeal court ordered a retrial and the man was acquitted.

CHILDREN IN COURT
The sometimes inhumane routine of the courts appears in sharpest relief in their treatment of children. A court room even for an adult is a rather frightening place: for a child it is almost nightmarish. Say a girl of eight has been molested. She is suddenly transported from her friends and playthings into a very sombre place which looks like a cross between a church and a classroom, which is enough to give you the jitters even without anybody in it. But there *are* people in it, although they are hardly recognizable as such: they are all wearing fancy dress and suddenly she is the focus of all attention. The Judge will ask her very solemnly if she knows what the truth is before she gives her evidence and she has to promise to tell it. She can see the accused person; he may be a friend of the family, or even a relative

— in cases of incest, her own father — and if the allegations are true this can only be a traumatic experience for the child. She may then be subjected to prying questions by the accused's barrister who will probably ask her the most intimate details of what actually happened and where the man groped her and so forth. Of course, it is the barrister's duty to do the best for his client and he will usually ask the child if she has ever told lies. The child being usually honest, will naïvely reply 'sometimes'. And from that moment on she is on the slippery slope and given a quite unexpected grilling. Is justice being served by this pantomime?

I realize that false or mistaken accusations are often made, but why not, as in America, have everybody sit round a table in an ordinary room in plain clothes? Let the child sit next to her mother or another adult with whom she feels comfortable. While it is one of our tenets that justice should be seen to be done and that therefore the defendant has a right to see witnesses as they give evidence, this can still be arranged by using a two-way mirror so that the child needn't be inhibited by the presence of a man who may be proved to have been her attacker or molester.

It has been estimated that one child in ten is sexually abused at one time or another. In America, according to S. Kraizer (*The Safe Child Book*, Futura 1986) the average molester of little girls molests 62 victims altogether and the molester of boys assaults 30 victims. Ten per cent of molesters are adult females ...

Room for improvement?

LET'S CHANGE THE SYSTEM
I ask myself whether the whole system isn't in need of radical reform. You've probably read of the astronomic costs of lawsuits today, and they are going up all the time. If the parties are legally aided the ultimate cost is borne by you and me, that is if you are a taxpayer, as I am. Even if they are not, the salaries of the court officials including the Judges have to be met, and these of course come from State funds. One of the reasons costs are so high is the time

spent on trying the matter: because of the way the evidence and submissions of counsel for the parties concerned all have to be listened to at length, it can take days if not weeks.

A number of Judges themselves, I'm flattered to say, agree with me. Mr Justice Caulfield has complained publicly that time and public money are being wasted in the Queen's Bench Division of the High Court because lawyers are not doing their bit to ensure an efficient flow of cases. He says 'the loss to the public purse is obviously very large'. Another senior Judge, Lord Justice Lawton, is on record (The Times, 6 December 1984) as saying: 'the administration of justice is being impeded by overlong trials and public funds are being wasted. Fashions in advocacy have changed, and in the last 30 years there has been a change from conciseness to prolixity. There must be a change back and quickly.' He was hearing an appeal to decide whether the jury had been unfairly overburdened with detailed evidence, the long speeches of counsel, the Judge's summing up (which went on for five days), the length of the trial (82 working days) and the conditions in which they sat and so on. The trial had cost the public £314,800 in legal fees, jury and witness expenses and the renting of the court. He voiced the view of his fellow Judges that they could not see the need for long opening nor long closing speeches by counsel, nor long summings up.

Lord Devlin, who had presided over some of the most important cases in British history, retired from the Bench at the age of 58 to the surprise of the legal establishment. He has only recently said why. He went to the House of Lords from the Court of Appeal because he found the appellate court utterly boring. He thought the move to the Lords would be better but it was worse. 'For the most part the work was dreary beyond belief' (The Times, 11 June 1985). He had found the appellate procedure absolutely stultifying. 'I thought the whole process was wrong. This interminable oral argument is a great waste of time.' He goes on to say that he has consistently called for a system in which the Judges read all the papers beforehand, including the barristers' submissions on the law, so that the oral proceedings in court are kept to a minimum, limited to testing, probing and clarifying the written arguments. 'My feeling on law reform has always been that it is the procedure more than the substantive law that needs alteration', he concluded. And who should know better?

CAPITAL PUNISHMENT
It's strange how some of the greatest law reforms have been brought about by one-man campaigns. The names that spring to mind are A.P. Herbert with divorce, David Steel with abortion — and Sidney Silverman with capital punishment. I knew Sidney Silverman quite well — in fact, I bought his house in Hampstead and we brought up our family there. It suffered from incurable subsidence (the house, I mean) which Sidney Silverman told me quite seriously in 1966 was 'actionable'. But since the house was built in 1936 and started to keel over almost at once, I think even Sidney Silverman would have had a problem suing the architect after 30 years of inertia. Another case of the cobbler not mending his own shoes.

But inertia was the last word to apply to Sidney Silverman in Parliament. As a man he was tiny — but then, so is a stick of dynamite. Single-handed he pushed through a bill abolishing the death penalty in 1965. Well, not quite. You can still be 'hanged by the neck until dead' for treason and a couple of other offences. In fact until relatively recently, under the Treason Act of 1814, the Sovereign, if he or she thought fit, could 'declare it to be (her) will and pleasure ... that the head shall be ... severed from the body of such persons whilst alive'. In plain English you could literally have got the chop for treason. You will be relieved to learn that this part of the Act is now repealed, although the hanging arrangements still stand.

You don't need a lot of imagination to know what treason is. But in case you don't, it's all spelt out in the Treason Act of 1351(!) which the House of Lords in 1946 took as its authority to confirm the death sentence on

William Joyce, known as Lord Haw-Haw, who made propaganda broadcasts to Britain in the service of the Nazis in the Second World War. His was the last death sentence for treason. He strenuously argued that he had given up British nationality when he went to live and work in Germany before the war, but got hooked on a technicality. Just before war broke out Joyce renewed his passport and he was hoist with his own petard. The Lords (not unanimously) ruled that by holding a British passport he 'claimed the protection of the Crown, and pledged the continuance of his fidelity'. If he had jacked it in he would have saved his neck and probably have become a chat-show host on the telly in the fullness of time, it being the British custom to revere old men and forgive them their trespasses.

By the way, you're guilty of treason if, among other things, you 'slay the Chancellor ... or the king's justices, being in their places doing their offices'. Chancellor means 'Lord Chancellor', so Lord Hailsham's person is adequately protected, but Nigel Lawson's isn't, though this doesn't mean that you can take a pot shot at him after the Budget. You just won't have to swing for it if you do.

As I have made clear, the Treason Act of 1351 can still be invoked. At the time of the Brighton bombings by Irish terrorists in 1984, when we almost lost the whole of the Cabinet, Lord Denning pointed out that if and when the terrorists were caught they could be dispatched quite legally and without any trouble under the provisions of this Act. However when McGee and his accomplices were caught they received prison sentences as was expected.

The other offences for which you can still be topped are piracy at sea with violence and (under the Dockyard etc. Protection Act 1772) setting fire to the Queen's ships or 'any ... military, naval or victualling stores'. Old soldiers will remember with affection, if not exactly relish, the 'cup of char and a wad' (a cup of tea and a sandwich) always available at the NAAFI in the dark days of the forties; now the Army doesn't do things by halves. I read in the papers that a secret cache of a million tins of Vim was recently found in the recesses of the War Office. And I don't think

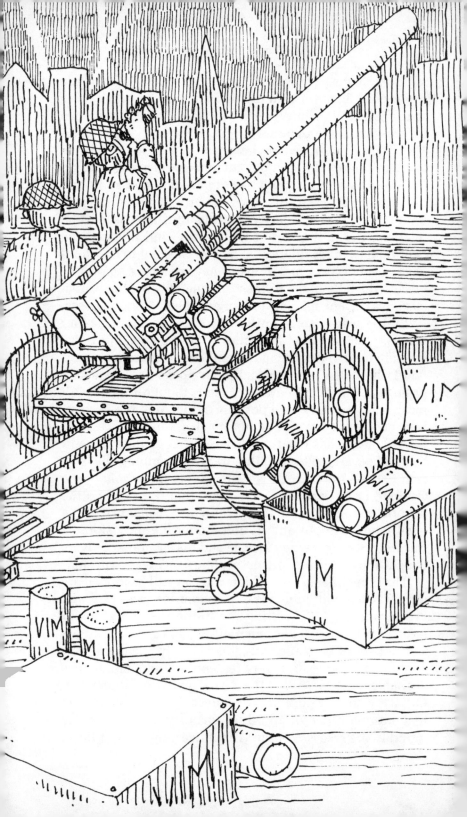

it will be long before archaeologists find an immense store of sandwiches amassed in case of emergency by the NAAFI. It's quite clear to me where the EEC got their ideas on building up food mountains. Now if you get bugged by all this if and when the sandwiches store is found, and you put a match to it in the interests of posterity, technically the 1772 Act will still prevail. It's not really worth a light is it?

There is, by the way, a set of gallows still in existence — at Wandsworth Prison in London. I had an interesting chat with the deputy governor and asked him if it was a museum piece and collecting dust or whether it was being properly looked after. He assured me that it was in full working order and periodically checked. It appears that the Chief Architect's department at the Home Office is responsible for the specifications and construction of gallows. I rang them. They told me that enquiries still come in from the Commonwealth for assistance. Why, only the other day an enquiry had been received from the Works Department at the Cayman Islands for help in disposing of some hapless inmates of the local nick. Intrigued, I put through a call to the Chief Engineer in the Cayman Islands who put my mind at rest. There had been a change of heart following the recent elections and the nefarious plans of the previous administration had been frustrated. I was also told there was a gallows in operation at St Helier, Jersey, but the governor of the prison there, Mr K. Wheeler, assures me that they were dismantled some years ago and he enterprisingly used the timbers to make a floor for the general stores of the prison. I am pleased to see that nothing is wasted in the prison service and the original gallows are now serving some socially useful purpose although, of course, there may be many who think they served a more useful purpose in days gone by.

Finally, if it comes to the pinch there is one certain way you can escape the gallows. If you are an expectant mother, a sentence of death cannot be passed on you under the provisions of The Sentence of Death (Expectant Mothers) Act 1931. This leniency goes back a long way and you will find quite a lot about it in Defoe's *Moll Flanders* (1722). It was called 'Pleading the Belly'. In our own day the Brazilian authorities refused to extradite Ronald Biggs, the train robber, on the grounds that he was an expectant father. It is heartening to see that liberal attitudes still persist in that paternalistic society.

LAUGHTER IN COURT

Our Judges, bless 'em, seem to have quaint notions of what is or is not an undeniable fact. If I am in court and say 'it's a well known fact that the Rolling Stones are a leading pop group' he is likely to say 'Who are or what are the Rolling Stones?' and 'What is a pop group?' This is because the Judge has no 'judicial notice' of the matter, that is he has not heard evidence in court to prove who or what the Rolling Stones are. And it does make some Alice in Wonderland sense, up to a point. Some years ago there was a music hall comedian called George Robey who was the Benny Hill of his day. A barrister was misguided enough to mention his name in a trial being heard by Lord Darling, a famous Judge and extrovert who prided himself on his witty interruptions of counsel in full flow. He pulled up the barrister and asked 'Who is George Robey?' The barrister with some presence of mind replied at once 'I believe they call him the darling of the halls, m'lud'.

This sort of judicial ignorance still persists, although to give the Bench some credit there are a number of legal presumptions which are regarded as irrefutable. These are curiously called 'notorious' facts. One of the meanings of 'notorious' as given in the OED is simply 'well-known' or 'forming a matter of common knowledge' (although if you refer to Margaret Thatcher or Neil Kinnock as being notorious politicians I somehow don't think this would be to their liking). However, if notorious facts are brought up in court the Bench accepts them without question. Here are a few of them. You will see that the courts do not take too much for granted. Judges have now decided that:
— 'A fortnight is too short a period for a pregnancy' (Preston-Jones v. Preston-Jones). In fact, inconceivable.

— 'The advancement of learning is among the purposes for which the University of Oxford exists' (Oxford Rate). Debatable.

— 'Cats are kept for domestic purposes' (Mye v. Niblatt). This reminds me of the old legal joke — I must tell it as there are so few of them — of the man up before the Judge for misbehaving with his dog. 'This is such a dreadful offence', said his lordship, 'I really don't know what to do with you'. Voice from the back of the court: 'Give him the cat!'

— 'The streets of London are full of traffic' (Dennis v. A.J. White and Co.) And the pavements full of dog droppings, as inhabitants of Barking, Essex, will testify. The Home Office has earmarked £10,000 to clean up the borough.

— 'The value of money has declined since 1189' (Bryant v. Foot). A remark of sterling worth.

— 'Astrology is balderdash' (Penny v. Hanson). A judgement from the Star Chamber?

— 'Whisky is intoxicating' (R. v. Nelson). Although a remark in the right spirit, I think most distillers would like to scotch this rumour.

— 'The life of a criminal is an unhappy one' (Burns v. Edman). The Judge actually said this in 1970 when he reduced the compensation to be paid to the widow of a criminal brought to an untimely end in a road accident. The normal figure for loss of expectation of life would have been £500 but the Judge cut this down to £250, as he didn't think the victim of the accident would have lived as happily as a law-abiding citizen would have done. I think a burglar's life has much to commend it: he is self-employed and most of his gains are tax-free, if he is good at his work he may end up with the glittering prize of a villa in Marbella.

I think Gilbert and Sullivan had it right in *The Pirates of Penzance*:

> When a felon's not engaged in his employment
> Or maturing his felonious little plans
> His capacity for innocent enjoyment
> Is just as great as any honest man's.

10

MISCELLANY

AN A TO Z OF LEGAL FICTIONS AND FALLACIES
All is fair in love and war. As to war, the Geneva
Convention has put a legal stop to this, as the Nazi leaders
found to their cost after the Second World War. As to love,
see 'Seduction is not a criminal offence' on page 185.
Assembly at school, you needn't have a religious. You
must. The 1944 Education Act says 'unless a pupil's
parents specifically object, the school day must start
with collective worship on the part of all pupils'. But
only 6 per cent of secondary schools do, so 94 per
cent break the law, according to a recent report in *The
Times.*

Benefit of clergy. A lot of people think that if they were
married in a register office and not in a church they were
married without 'benefit of clergy'. This is a
misconception. Benefit of clergy has a very restricted
meaning. It was a right you could claim in the old days
for exemption from trial by a secular court, if you could
read, and preferred to be tried by a *church* court, which
was much more lenient (see page 109).
Bite, every dog is allowed one. Not true. If you know your
dog is dangerous, even though he hasn't bitten anybody
yet, you could be in trouble. If you put a notice up on your
door saying 'Beware of the Dog' you are telling everybody
you know your dog is dangerous, and if he bites the
postman you may have to pay up.
*Broker, if you lose money on an insurance policy through
a broker's bad advice you can't get your money back from
your.* You can. This was done successfully after the
Signal Life disaster in 1982. But don't expect any help from
the official bodies (see page 200).

Cautions by the police.   It is generally thought that when a policeman cautions you he ends up by saying '... anything you say may be taken down in evidence and used against you'. If he says 'against you' this is quite wrong. The evidence may be in your favour, but the implication of his words is that he has made up his mind that you are guilty.

Common law wife.   This is not a legal term, although often used mistakenly as such. The law speaks of a common law *marriage* which is a marriage celebrated in a place where the local ceremonies are unacceptable to you or non-existent, when you can declare yourself wed by 'an informal exchange of consent'. But the expression 'common law wife', as used today means the exact opposite, referring to a woman living with a man who has not gone through any form of marriage ceremony and doesn't want to. The correct term is 'mistress' or 'cohabitee' (ugh).

Comparisons are odious.   Barristers and Judges don't think so, as they are always comparing your case with previous similar cases when you are on trial.

Crime does not pay.   There are a number of gentlemen in Marbella who would beg leave to disagree, and it would be hard to contradict them.

Corpse, to prove murder there has to be a.   Not on your life. There have been many convictions without a corpse having been found. (The Latin words *corpus delicti* are often misused to refer to the body in the case of murder. It is in fact a legal term referring to the essential acts and facts which constitute a crime.)

Debt, you can't be imprisoned any more for.   Originally, if someone owed you money you could have him locked up even if it was for a trivial sum. The Debtors Act 1860 put a stop to this — almost. You can still be put in jug for certain debts to the State. A dissident Quaker recently refused to pay his income tax on grounds of conscience in that he didn't want any of his money to go towards the manufacture of weapons of mass destruction, and he got fourteen days. Ah, you say, I can see that. But did you know you can still be put inside for not paying your ex-wife arrears of maintenance? This is technically because you are in contempt of court. And it's more common than you think.

Exchange *is no robbery.*   Technically, this is correct since robbery involves the use, or threat of force. Taking it in its ordinary meaning it's misleading; for example if you give a five pound note for a box of chocolates in a sweet shop and the assistant makes a mistake and gives you change for a £10 note and you notice it and don't do anything about it, you are guilty of theft.

Fair *cop guv'nor, it's a.*   I understand these words are no longer used by professional criminals but only, if at all, by enthusiastic and incompetent amateurs.

God *is always on the side of the big battalions.*   Not necessarily any more with the advent of legal aid.
God, *so help me.*   'I ... promise to tell the truth, the whole truth, and nothing but the truth. So help me God.' This used to be the form of the oath you had to take in court but reference to divine assistance has now gone by the board.

Honour *among thieves.*   I ask you.

Insulting *behaviour leading to a breach of the peace, you can always be had up for.*   As a matter of fact, and really of law, you can never be charged with this offence against the police. Why not? Because it seems that the very status of a police officer as one who guards the peace makes it impossible for him to be provoked into breaking it.
'*I promise to pay the bearer on demand the sum of* £1/5/10/20/50. *Signed, D.H.F. Somerset, Chief Cashier, Bank of England*'.   You will see these words on all bank notes. Try ringing up Mr Somerset to get him to honour his promise — in gold.

Judge, as sober as a.   Hmmm.

Judges take no part in politics.   Many Judges are in the House of Lords and speak out on proposed legislation which can be quite controversial. Even more so in the House of Commons where there are quite a few MPs who are Recorders (that is, minor Judges).

King can do no wrong, the.   This is meant in the legal, not moral, sense but is hardly true. I refer you to the Crown Proceedings Act 1947, which gives the Crown immunity from all sorts of violations of the law. A.P. Herbert has pointed out that by the Crown, although 'we sometimes mean the Monarch herself we more often mean the government or some Department of it or some department of some Department, and sometimes in practice, some subordinate clerk in some department of some Department'. This was brought into sharp focus when hospital kitchens were found to be in such a disgraceful state that they were a threat to the health of the patients. A small step has been taken to remove this particular immunity, but it is only a small step and not exactly a giant leap for mankind. Members of the armed services are still very badly treated if they're involved in an accident or left paralysed after an operation carried out by an Army medic; the compensation they're given is niggardly compared to what they would get if this immunity was done away with.

Lord Privy Seal.   This is like the Holy Roman Empire which was neither holy, Roman, nor an empire, and the phrase 'Your obedient servant'. It is a government ministerial post, and usually combined with the office of the Leader of the House of Commons. The present incumbent is Mr John Biffen who is neither a lord, nor a privy, nor a seal.

Master of a ship can marry you, the.   Not at all. This is a Hollywood myth. Captains of ships and aircraft have no authority whatsoever to pronounce you man and wife. The only splicing they can do is that of the mainbrace.

Man proposes, *God disposes.*   Not in our law courts, where the Judge is the supreme authority. An old lag up for drunkenness said to the Bench 'As God's my judge I'm not guilty of this offence, your honour'. The Judge, a bit short as you might imagine, replied, 'He's not. I am. You are. Three months.'

Marriages are made in heaven.   They're not. They have to be made at a register office or at a place specially licensed.

Murder will out.   Ring Scotland Yard and ask how many unsolved murders they've got on their files. You can get away with murder, literally.

Necessity knows no law.   Somebody said self-preservation is the first law of nature. It may be a law of nature but not the law of our country. If you kill somebody to eat them to stay alive after you've been shipwrecked, you're in trouble. See 'Cannibalism', page 196.

Obscenities at your boss, you can be sacked for shouting.   Not necessarily. In February 1974 the head gardener employed on a Lincolnshire estate used foul language to his employer and was sacked on the spot. The employer wrote to him 'there can be no question of remaining in my employment when you choose to use obscene four-letter words in the direct presence of my wife and children'. The Court of Appeal were very sympathetic to the employee since his boss 'had behaved in an arrogant manner and provoked a decent servant into the use of unseemly language'. They upheld the previous court's award of damages for wrongful dismissal. But I don't advise you to try this on the guv'nor.

Passports, the police can impound.   A popular myth which the police encourage. They can't do it arbitrarily, but only if it's materially relevant to the offence with which you are charged. See page 127. While we're on the powers of the police, another popular fallacy is that they can take you into custody for questioning. They cannot. Lord Devlin, one of our most eminent Judges, scotched that one. 'You may sometimes read in novels and detective stories,' he said, 'that persons are sometimes taken into custody for questioning. There is no such power in this country. A man cannot be detained unless he is arrested.' While this celebrated civil liberty has been somewhat dented by the Police and Criminal Evidence Act 1984, in that you can be taken in to be searched if it is thought you have evidence of stolen property or suchlike on you, it otherwise remains a basic right of every citizen. Nor can the police take you into custody to 'assist with enquiries'. If you are merely 'helping police with their enquiries', you can just get up and walk out. If they try to stop you, they are assaulting you (unless they arrest you first).

Possession *is nine points of the law.* I don't know what meaning this phrase has, legal or otherwise. Certainly the mere act of possession of any property does not give you any legal title to it. Much on a par with 'what's mine is mine, and what's yours is also mine'.

Quit, *notice to.* You may think that if you go through the legal rigmarole of serving a notice to quit on a tenant he has to comply with it. Not at all. Nobody can be made to leave their home by the landlord, if he doesn't want to, without a court order.

Rape, *if a man forces his wife to have sex with him he can be had up for.* Generally speaking he can't, except possibly in Scotland. See page 39.

Seduction *is not a criminal offence.* It can be. If you use the fuddle-duddle method and fill your partner up with drink so that she doesn't know whether she's coming or going and have your way with her, you can be charged with rape. There are decided cases on it. As T.S. Eliot has written:
> *When lovely woman stoops to folly and*
> *Paces about her room again, alone,*
> *She smoothes her hair with automatic hand,*
> *And puts a record on the gramophone.*

That is, before she rings the police to report you.

Tattooed, *anybody can be.* No they can't. It's an offence to tattoo a person under the age of 18, except for medical reasons, and then it must be by a doctor or a person under his direction. A special Act of Parliament was brought in to prevent this (Tattooing of Minors Act 1969). It is a defence for anyone charged to show he thought a tattooee was over 18.

Trespassers *will be prosecuted.* Ah, we all know this one. Or do we? Trespass is a civil offence, and you can only be prosecuted for a *criminal* offence. But in certain cases a trespasser *can* be prosecuted — if he is a poacher, for instance, a gamekeeper has the power to arrest him for the criminal offence of infringing his employer's game rights.

Usury. It has been said that usury is murder. If it is, I know a lot of bank managers who should be behind bars.

Variation *Order, if I'm divorced and my ex and I agree to up or cut her maintenance payments, to get tax relief we have to go to a solicitor and to court for a.* You don't. All you have to do if you're the one doing the paying is write out a simple declaration and sign it in front of a witness. Best to send it first to your local taxman for him to approve. I did this myself and it worked like a charm.

Virtue *is its own reward.* Not so. An informer will often get a reward if he splits on his accomplices, and if he turns state evidence he will usually get off the book as well. It is more encouraging to see that courts often make a reward of money to a law-abiding citizen who has helped to catch a criminal.

Ways, *you can't have it both.* Nowadays you can. See 'Lex of Sex', page 32.
Will, *you gather in the solicitors office after the death of the loved one to read the.* A myth promoted by

Hollywood again. I've never read a will aloud in my life to the beneficiaries. In fact, the beneficiaries rarely see the will or know of its contents; the only person who does is the executor who normally has a copy of the will anyway. If he or she hasn't, I send him one. To plough through a will in the office with all its incomprehensible jargon would really put people off solicitors for life (if they weren't already).

Witness, a person has to read a document (such as a will) before he signs it as a. Not at all. The job of a witness is just to attest your signature on a document, i.e. certify it was you who signed it. But he must be somebody who knows you, such as a neighbour or the milkman, so that he can say so afterwards if need be (for example if it's claimed after you die leaving all your money to the cat's home that the will was forged).

X-perience is the best teacher. Eh? Just see how many criminals have previous convictions, and that goes for solicitors too (who shouldn't have any convictions of course), who will time and again forget to ask for something on account from clients they know to be notoriously slow payers.

Year and a day, to be charged with murder or manslaughter the victim must die within a. True. But this does not apply to statutory forms of homicide such as infanticide and causing death by dangerous driving.

Zany, the law isn't. WHAT?

TAX

THE WAGES OF SIN — ARE TAXABLE
In the eyes of the Inland Revenue a burglar, or any criminal for that matter, is assessable for tax on his income and capital gains, whether from the proceeds of crime or otherwise. I have this on authority from the horse's mouth, namely the Technical Division of the Inland Revenue at

Somerset House, who advise me that 'the profits of all trades are taxable regardless of whether the trades themselves, or particular aspects of them, are illegal.' There are (what did you expect?) only a few reported cases. In 1932 (Mann v. Nash) profits from the illegal use of fruit machines were held to be taxable. Street betting is still illegal and if you are caught you have to pay tax, as the Judge held in the case of Southern v. A.B. Ltd (1933), when he said 'the burglar and the swindler ... are as liable to tax as an honest business man, and in addition, they get their deserts elsewhere'.

Prostitution, as I have said elsewhere in this book, is not itself a crime. It is a legitimate vocation and thus quite clearly taxable. Running a brothel *is* a criminal offence, and a madam has to fill in her tax returns otherwise she's for it.

Gambling, which some may regard as sinful, whilst strictly controlled by the law, is not illegal, although it used to be. Cards, dice, cock-fighting and races were all once illegal (cock-fighting still is, but for different reasons) and you were 'a rogue and vagabond' if you engaged in them. In the fourteenth century Edward III even banned football because he thought his subjects should be more interested in the 'noble sports of war'. Quite a change from Edward VII, who came to be known as the sporting king and followed the horses ardently, a royal pastime which has endured to this day. Her Majesty's Inspectors of the Inland Revenue share these sporting interests and brought an action in 1925 (Graham v. Green) to recover tax from a skilful punter who habitually but not deceitfully fleeced the bookies (well done, that man). Mr Green was allowed to hold on to his winnings as he did not 'carry on a trade'. So if your little flutters bring you rich rewards, even though you do it year in and year out, you don't pay any tax. You get off scot-free ('scot' being the old word for tax; it is also connected with the word 'shot', as when you pay your shot for a round of drinks, but not related to a 'shot in the giblets' which means pregnant). But be warned. You can't deduct betting losses from your income when you fill in your tax returns, just as you can't parking fines, etc.

On the other hand, while tax evasion is quite properly a criminal offence, tax *avoidance* is a legitimate occupation. Indeed it is often a preoccupation for many of us, and provides tax lawyers and accountants with a good living, although the income they may derive from this pursuit, huge as it may be, is not to be compared with the money they save their clients. For the Vestey family, who made their vast fortune from selling meat, the tax lawyers certainly brought home the bacon. The tax the Vesteys paid over the years on their millions was so insignificant due to loopholes in the law that it caused an uproar in Parliament, and the law had to be changed. Who says we don't need lawyers?

ENTERTAINMENTS TAX — KEEPING ABREAST OF THE LAW

If you think Her Majesty's Inspectors of the Inland Revenue are heartless monsters, you ain't seen nuthin' yet, in the words of a famous American President. The journal of the American tax accountants, the *Taxation Record*, reported some years ago the case of an American barmaid. Apparently in the USA there is an additional tax on refreshments served in hotel and restaurants when entertainment is provided. This particular lady was endowed with considerable talents. In fact she could balance up to four glasses of beer on her bust whilst serving customers. This attracted the attention of the American taxman who claimed that the behaviour of the lady in question was ample proof that she was providing an entertainment within the meaning of their tax laws. Her employers had to pay up. Let it be said that when this assessment was announced the American drinking community took the barmaid to *their* bosom.

FINDERS KEEPERS?

Another complex area of the law. Let's have a quiz. What is your position if:

1. you find a wad of fivers in a second-hand wardrobe you've bought from a dealer, or in the pocket of a suit you picked up at a jumble sale?
2. you find a wallet in the street?
3. you find a wallet in the loo at Harrods?
4. you are given change for £5 at the sweetshop when you only gave £1 for what you bought?
5. you live in a rented flat and open a disused cupboard where you find a Queen Anne silver tea service?
6. you are digging in your garden, or beachcombing with your metal detector, and strike gold in the form of a hoard of Roman coins? When you examine them you see that some are indeed gold, some silver and the rest copper, with some pretty diamond clasps.
7. you are employed by a company to clean out a pool on land owned by them and find two gold rings?
8. you are waiting in the passenger lounge at Heathrow airport and spot a gold bracelet on the floor of the lounge? You pick it up and hand it in, asking for it to be sent to you if it's not claimed. You find a few months later that British Airways have sold it and held on to the money.

The general principle is that unless an owner deliberately abandons something that belongs to him he always retains his title of ownership. If he can't be traced, the finder may keep the property, provided it was found in a 'public' place, such as the street. If you find it in a 'private' place, such as somebody's home or in a shop, it generally belongs to the occupier of the premises, although surprisingly it may depend on which side of the counter the item was found. If you know who the true owner is and keep the property without saying anything you commit theft, which is, of course, a criminal offence.

Treasure trove is in a class of its own. Trove comes from the French word *trouvé* (meaning 'found'), but it only applies to gold and silver of unknown ownership hidden in the earth which you dig up, and it always belongs to the Crown. If you report it to the police, as you are supposed to, and the authorities regard it of historical interest and want it for a museum or suchlike you will be

paid its full market value. If you don't report it, you're in trouble because your find will be confiscated and you may be prosecuted. The penalties are a fine or imprisonment, with no fixed maximum. If it turns out after all that it doesn't come within the category of treasure trove, then it belongs to the owner of the land on which it was found.

So the answers to the quiz are as follows:

1. The money belongs to the original owner, unless it was intended to be left in the wardrobe or suit (very doubtful) when sold to the dealer or given to the jumble sale. It must be returned.

2. Ditto. You should hand it in to the police. But you can claim it after six months.

3. Ditto, possibly. It belongs to Harrods if the owner doesn't come forward — or does it? Was it found in a 'public' or a 'private' place? Still a grey area, but see answer to no. 8.

4. The over-payment to you was a mistake, and the surplus clearly belongs to the shopkeeper. If you don't hand it back you are guilty of theft. This also applies when there is a 'bank error in your favour' and you 'collect £200' or more. If you know and you don't tell the bank you not only do not pass 'Go' but also, theoretically, you can 'Go to jail'.

5. You must give it to the owner of the property from whom you rent the flat. He has a better claim to it.

6. This is a trick question. The gold and silver are treasure trove and belong to the Crown. The rest belongs to you. (Att.-Gen. of the Duchy of Lancaster v. G.E. Overton Farms, 1982) Archaeologists are miffed by the current state of the law, as they think, with some justice, that *all* ancient loot should be classed as treasure trove.

7. This was an actual case (South Staffordshire Water Company v. Sharman, 1896), when the company got the rings since they owned the land. When you buy land you buy everything that's on, over or under it, so if you strike oil in your garden, or find there is a rich vein of tin under it, it all belongs to you unless the previous owner reserved the mineral rights to himself, as is often the case in coal-mining areas.

8. Again an actual case (Parker v. British Airways Board, 1982). The bracelet was found in a 'public' place (the lounge) and Mr Parker had a better right to it than the airline, who had the effrontery to go to the Court of Appeal where they were soundly trounced. Mr Parker got the money they had pocketed *plus* interest, and quite right, too.

What happens if you find something and hand it in at the local police station, assuming the owner can't be found and you don't want to lay claim to it at all? The article is auctioned and the money goes to police funds.

Will you get a reward (as is the law in some other countries) for returning lost property to the owner? This is entirely up to the owner. You have no right to insist on any reward or compensation, and if you're the one who lost the watch or wallet it's an offence to advertise for its return saying 'No questions asked'. If a reward has been offered, you must pay it to anyone who meets the conditions stated in the offer.

And a final sardonic conundrum: you are a solicitor in partnership with Mr B. A little old lady comes in to pay your bill of £60 and gives you six notes, and only when she leaves do you see that two of them are £50 notes. That's an easy one, you say. Oh no it's not. The problem is *do you tell your partner?* (that's an old legal joke solicitors tell against themselves).

CITIZEN'S ARREST

Can you arrest your next-door neighbour, or the milkman, or your wife or husband? I don't mean call in the police to arrest them, I mean can you as a private individual arrest them and march them off to the local lockup? You certainly can, but only in special circumstances. Any citizen has this right and it's called a citizen's arrest. Just as a policeman can arrest someone without a warrant if the person is seen or suspected of committing an 'arrestable offence', so can you. There is a long list of arrestable offences which include theft, drug offences, demanding money with menaces (this used to be called blackmail), burglary, rape and so on. Store detectives, for instance, can arrest people they believe to be shoplifting. You must be reasonable about it of course, and if the person you arrest turns out to be blameless you may be sued for damages for false imprisonment.

You can also arrest anybody for 'breach of the peace', particularly if it looks as though some physical violence will ensue, but you should only attempt this as a last resort. Could be nasty. However, if a policeman calls upon you to help him if he is obstructed when making an arrest for breach of the peace, you *must* assist him. If you don't you will be guilty of a criminal offence yourself, even if your help would have been useless (Criminal Law Act 1967 Section 5(3)).

These are called 'common law' powers of arrest, as distinct from 'statutory' powers. Common law in this context means basically the law as pronounced by Judges over the centuries in individual cases, the rulings in which are called 'precedents' and become almost sacred. 'Statutory' law means what it says, namely the law as codified by statutes, that is, simply, Acts of Parliament. There are a number of specific *statutory* powers of arrest which we all have. Among these are powers to arrest:
— a man found persistently soliciting in a public place for immoral purposes
— anyone found living on the earnings of *male* prostitution
— anyone reasonably suspected of committing an offence under the Official Secrets Acts
— anyone reasonably suspected of going equipped for burglary, theft or cheat
— anyone reasonably suspected of going absent without leave from the armed forces
— anyone found drunk in certain circumstances.

You will be interested to know that there are certain persons apart from the police who have specific statutory powers of arrest for other offences. These are:
— a churchwarden, if you make a nuisance of yourself in church, whether during a service or otherwise (Ecclesiastical Courts Juristiction Act 1860 Section 3)
— a pawnbroker, if you offer him an article he reasonably thinks has been pinched

— the captain of a ship in certain circumstances
— the captain of a UK aircraft if he has reasonable grounds for thinking you have done something on board the plane while in flight which is a serious offence in the UK
— a gamekeeper if you are a trespasser and you don't give him your name and address for a summons to be served
— any member of the armed forces if you are reasonably thought to be guilty of an offence under the Customs and Excise Acts.

CANNIBALISM

Eating people is not wrong in the eyes of the law in the UK, but it is an offence to kill them first and then eat them. I believe Mr Norman Tebbitt is on record as saying he would have Mr Neil Kinnock for breakfast, but since they probably give each other indigestion anyway I don't really think he would go that far. It is an offence to do away with somebody to put them on your menu even if you may die yourself if you don't eat them. Some years ago when an aircraft crashed in the Andes the few survivors only managed to hang on by tucking into one or two of the dead passengers, and they were not subject to any legal charges.

It is quite different, however, if you are shipwrecked and to prevent yourself dying of starvation you decide to make a meal of the cabin boy and do him in for the purpose. These were the facts in R. v. Dudley and Stephens (1884) when the Chief Justice at the time, Lord Coleridge, took a dim view of the two mariners who made the poor lad their dish of the day. He couldn't accept the defence that 'necessity knows no law'. There were no decided cases to go on. An American case (US v. Holmes 1842) had been cited to show that 'sailors had no right to throw passengers overboard to save themselves'. Indeed, they should be the first to go because of the duty of protection owed to passengers. In this case Holmes, a member of the crew adrift in an open boat which was too full to remain afloat, chucked not just one but a *number* of the passengers overboard. He was awarded six months and a fine of $20. Lord Coleridge and his fellow Judges considered it was poor form for Dudley and Stephens to do away with the cabin boy and sentenced them to death for murder. But this was later commuted to six months in the choky. Strangely no comment was made about eating human flesh.

Well, cannibalism has a long pedigree. The word comes from Carib, the name of a tribe (now extinct) in the West Indies, and the name lives on in the 'Caribbean'. At some time or other this aberration has been practised almost everywhere, including Ireland and Scotland (having sampled haggis I can see why) and Australia.

Gastronomical note I understand from those in the know that the considered preference of most cannibals at table is for the palm of the hand and the testicles, which are far superior to live monkeys' brains. But you won't get them in London, even at Fortnum and Mason, since they no longer go so far as to stock chocolate-covered bumble-bees and grasshoppers in syrup. The best they can do for you at the moment is 50 grammes of snails' eggs (at £32.50).

INSURANCE

Let's play Twenty Questions. Before you start to yawn, let me tell you, the subject is fascinating. I could write a book on it. In fact, I *am* writing a book on it. I find that the man in the street is baffled by money. Even people who should know better approach the subject with some reserve, if not distaste, and one of the definitions of a gentleman is 'someone who doesn't count his change'. And like death they don't like talking about it.

Maybe we're no longer a nation of gentlemen, for I'm pleased to say that this aloof attitude seems to be changing. But not much. While we may check the change we get for a pound note (sorry, coin), we still accept with touching trust what we're told by banks and building societies and insurance companies whose impressive offices and logos on their notepaper suggest infallibility and complete reliability. I do a lot of conveyancing. Most clients have a mortgage on the house or flat they're selling and this has to be redeemed, that is, paid off, on the day of completion.

I therefore ask the building society for a 'redemption' statement calculated to the day of completion, and I get one saying, for example, that £24,332.44 will be needed by them to discharge, i.e. cancel, the mortgage. I pass this figure on to the client, who never questions it, accepting it as gospel. I think all building societies are computerized nowadays, but don't tell me they never make mistakes. And this goes for insurance companies too.

I have to restrain myself on insurance otherwise this chapter will go on for several hundred pages. I'm just going to ask the insurance industry twenty questions, and maybe these will give you something to think about.

Before I do, let me tell you a story. When somebody dies leaving a life policy, the insurance company will only pay out the proceeds on production of what is called a grant of probate, or letters of administration. All right and proper. You may know it can take months to get such a grant; on average it takes three months, but this is no fault of the insurance company, nor of the solicitor handling your affairs. This sort of delay is in the nature of things. When the company finally gets the grant it pays up almost at once. But what about *interest* on the money in the meantime? The majority of companies don't pay you any, and the money you forfeit can be substantial. Let's put it in figures. Joe Bloggs dies on 1 January with a life policy of £40,000 (not uncommon). The company pays out £40,000 on 1 April. If they had paid out on the day of his death you could have invested this money, at say 10 per cent per annum, and earned £1,000 in interest in the quarter between 1 January and 1 April (10 per cent of £40,000 = £4,000, divided by 4 = £1,000). Most companies earn this sort of money themselves (if not more) and put it in their own pockets. I estimate that the total of such money kept by these companies is about £12 million per year. And who are the beneficiaries deprived of this money? Mainly, literally widows and orphans. There were 3.2 million widows here in 1984 and nine out of ten were pensioners, for whom every penny counts.

I thought this wasn't exactly cricket so I campaigned, single-handed, for things to be put right. After two years the bastions crumbled, and on 18 November 1985 the Secretary of State for Trade and Industry announced in the House of Commons that interest would in future be paid on policies after the death of the policyholder until the date of the pay-out. That was the good news. The bad news was that interest would not start to run until *two months* after the death of the policyholder with the result that the industry would *still* continue to withhold about £8 million a year. *The Times* wrote this up and spoke of a 'shoddy compromise', as indeed it was. So further changes in the law are still needed.

Now the 20 questions I would like answered by the insurance industry.

1.   Why can't interest be paid on *all* claims from the date of the claim to the date of the payout?

If someone has a car accident it may take up to six months before he gets paid. He may have to borrow money from the bank in the meantime to hire or buy another car, which can be costly. The companies say it would be too expensive and premiums would have to go sky-high. Why should they? Let's do some simple arithmetic. Total car claims in 1984 came to £1.6 billion. Say the average time to pay up takes three months. Claimants therefore lose a quarter of a year's interest, which at 10 per cent per annum comes to £40 million across the board (10 per cent of 1.6 billion = £160 million, divided by 4 = £40 million). There are 20 million licensed motors on the road, so if each motor policy was surcharged to pay for the extra expense of paying interest what would be the average increase per policy? You don't need to be an Einstein to see it comes to *only £2* per policy *per year* (£40 million interest divided by 20 million motors). Why can't it be done?

2.   Why not ban hype in the ads?

Mr Stewart Lyon, a past president of the Institute of Actuaries and thus no slouch, came out recently with a strong attack on his own colleagues in the insurance industry. Many of the illustrations of projected bonuses and profits on policies as currently advertised are 'pie in the sky', as he put it. I thought insurance was based on the principle of the utmost good faith between *both* parties, the policyholder and the insurance company.

3.   Why don't all insurance salesmen have to disclose the commission they earn on selling a policy for a pension, endowment, life or any other?

If you go to three different insurance brokers or salesmen asking for the best policy in your circumstances I bet you'll be recommended to three different companies. The reason is clear. It's very doubtful you will be guided to a company who don't pay any commission, and there are quite a few.

4.   Why do insurance companies pay commission at all when a policy is taken out? Why not let the *buyer* pay for disinterested advice?

If you go to a doctor or an accountant you don't expect to be prescribed a drug on which the doctor takes a cut, or to take certain action with your finances which will benefit the accountant. Just as the insurance industry has clubbed together to pay for an Ombudsman, why not tackle the problem at source and fund a policyholders' organization that would give objective advice, at least in principle, if not detail, on the 'bargains' offered by the industry?

If this is a counsel of perfection why not control the conduct of insurance salesmen, many of whom were selling double-glazing or sliced bread before they went into insurance to make a fast buck. As the law stands, *anyone* can sell life assurance provided they don't use the title of insurance broker. So they call themselves 'consultants', almost a dirty word today on a par with 'company director' or 'model'. They should all have to be licensed and cop it if they step out of line.

5.   Why not control the activities of all insurance *brokers* more closely?

The collapse of Signal Life in 1982 with a loss to 300 investors of £1.5 million met with apathy, so far as the losers were concerned, by the industry and, what is outrageous, by the very bodies supposed to help you in difficulties with insurance brokers, namely the Insurance Brokers Registration

Council and the British Insurance Brokers Association. John Potter quite understandably was appalled by their indifference and formed an action group. He was very successful and got the brokers to pay compensation for their negligence in giving bad advice. He is caustic about these bodies. He says 'The most depressing aspect of the whole affair is that the IBRC and BIBA have been absolutely useless, and if the public thinks that member-ship of these organizations is any protection for them, they are wrong. They have done nothing.' (*The Times*, 14 March 1986).

6. Why don't insurance companies point out that a policyholder benefits considerably by 'staggering' his premiums on a life policy?

I'll explain. If you have a motor or house policy and sell your car or home in the middle of the insurance year, you will get a pro rata refund of the annual premium that you have paid; not so with a life policy. Say you pay £600 once a year for a life policy. If you die a month after the renewal, your estate doesn't get any refund which theoretically amounts to £550 (eleven-twelfths of £600). This has the curious effect that a deceased policyholder is paying for life cover beyond the grave. If you pay premiums *monthly*, as you may, although they may be loaded by 10 per cent or thereabouts, you are still quids in when you die (!) since you will only have paid £55 and your estate will save £605.

But why not just give a pro rata refund automatically, as is the case in Switzerland, and some other countries?

7. The industry is not so keen on disclosing the commissions their salesmen collect. Why do they make applicants for policies disclose every single detail of their history, and disqualify them from claims later on for non-disclosure of an incident in their lives which has no bearing on the policy?

8. Why don't non-life policies make it perfectly clear that if you don't insure, say, the contents of your home for their correct value, that is if you're under-insured, you will only get paid out pro-rata on a claim?

for £10,000 but at the time of a claim they are worth
£20,000. A suite of furniture and your carpets are ruined
by a flood and you put in a claim for £2,000. You'll only
get half, i.e. £1,000 (this is what is called 'averaging').

By the way, you should note that damage to a carpet
by spilled paint is not covered under a standard policy.
9.   Why don't renewal notices say in *very bold print* that
any changes in values or circumstances must be notified
to the insurance company?

An insurance company will often wriggle out of a claim
by saying you didn't tell them this, that or the other.
10.   Why isn't it made abundantly clear in a household
policy that a claim will rarely be met for damage to a fence
or a boundary wall?

It is very rare for a household policy to cover the garden
itself. This should be available for an extra premium.
Subsidence and suchlike causing damage to a garden wall
will not give rise to a claim unless the main dwelling house
is damaged by the same cause at the same time. Why not?
At least this should be made clear in the policy.
11.   Why do insurance companies employ loss adjusters
whose earnings depend on their record of the amount of
money by which they reduce the claim, and who
sometimes make the claimant feel like a crook in the
process? Why not elevate the occupation of an adjuster to
that of a profession with decent standards of practice?
12.   If you are tricked into handing over a motor car
to a con-man in return for a forged cheque, why isn't
this considered as 'theft' within the terms of a motor
policy?
13.   If a friend who is not a member of your immediate
family leaves with you or lends to you an article that is
stolen, you can't claim. Why isn't this clear in the policy?
14.   Why don't motor policies highlight the fact that while
your comprehensive policy may say that you're insured
when driving another car, you're only insured, when so
driving, for third party claims?
Fire, theft and damage to the car are excluded.

15.   Why not give claim-free people a no-claim bonus every year as is the case with car insurance?

If I look after my property carefully I should not have to pay indirectly for someone who doesn't.

16.   Why are policies still written in gobbledegook?

The average policy is incomprehensible to the layman.

17.   In order that the terms of a policy may be fully understood why not allow 14 days cover (or more) on approval?

18.   Why isn't there a standard format for all insurance policies so that one could be compared with another easily to show what risks are covered and what are not?

I would like to see every policy supplied with a booklet explaining it *line by line* in simple English. At the end of 1984 there were 95.6 million life policies in force. God knows how many other policies there may be for other types of business — the figures aren't published.

19.   Why doesn't the insurance industry show some interest in the community apart from sponsoring sports matches and concerts, which are thinly disguised forms of advertising?

Have you ever heard of an insurance company funding research into flammable materials, or a tyre that doesn't puncture? You haven't? Neither have I. It could reduce accident claims enormously. Prevention is better than cure. The motor insurance business shows serious losses year after year; in 1983 the net loss was £114 million on premium income of £1,784 million, a worsening of losses of almost 50 per cent over 1982.

20.   Most companies support the Insurance Ombudsman. Why not all?

Better still, why not have a single independent body across the board to arbitrate between the policyholder and the insurer? Redress under Lloyds' policies is still very restricted. I really would like to see a national policyholders' association formed to look after all of us on the other side of the counter and to bring a bit of balance to what is often a one-sided transaction.

Phew. You may think I have a vendetta against the insurance industry. I don't. Some of my best friends are insurance brokers (outside their offices, of course). The strange thing is that the insurance industry has a good record on the whole. But it also has some tremendous shortcomings, as do other great financial institutions, such as banks and building societies, which should be put right by law. Self-regulation is all very well, but as a wise old headmaster of mine used to say 'There are no rules at this school until they are broken'.

The rules have been broken and the law should step in.

DRUGS

We have heard so much about drugs recently, so I shall try and keep this brief. Knowing the heartbreak to which main-line addiction can lead I would give pushers a life sentence; this could be done by a single amendment of the Misuse of Drugs Act 1971. But, as we all know, Acts of Parliament are just not enough to control all the evils in our society. Years ago it was said 'you can drive a coach and four through any law' and the same is true today. On TV recently the actor Joss Ackland described in a hour-long programme his son's addiction to heroin which led to his death. Everything started when his son — a boy of 9 or 10 — was found at a railway station, unconscious after having apparently been given a dozen Mandrax pills or capsules. In my view this should have been a red light for the parents, but it is not for me to point a finger. 'No man is an island ... any man's death diminishes me, because I am involved in mankind; and therefore never send to know for whom the bell tolls; it tolls for thee.' (John Donne).

Cannabis is very controversial. Napoleon didn't think much of it and banned it. James Callaghan thinks along the same lines and said so in 1969 when he urged Parliament 'to call a halt in the advancing tide of so-called permissiveness'. The drug is apparently controlled more stringently here than in most other countries, and convictions average over 10,000 per annum. On the other hand, there are many who see it as no more harmful than

alcohol. My own strong reservations are that the drug introduces young people to the twilight world of drug abuse and *may* be a stepping stone to untold misery.

TAKING POT LUCK

You know you mustn't grow cannabis in your house or garden. It may be cultivated only under licence from the Home Office and smoked only on approved premises. Further, it used to be an offence to attempt to commit, or to incite or attempt to incite another to commit the offence of cultivating it. The law has now changed by redefinition in the Criminal Attempts Act 1981, but you must still be very careful. If you say to somebody 'ever thought of growing pot? it's not a bad idea' you might be in trouble.

HAVING POT ON THE PREMISES

It is an offence to permit premises to be used for smoking cannabis.

SOME CASES OF DRUG POSSESSION

— in R. v. Frederich a conviction was upheld in the Appeal Court on the basis of 'traces' of cannabis being found in a pouch and pipes in a flat.

— similarly, in R. v. Graham police found traces in scrapings from Mr Graham's pockets. Since what was found could be measured and weighed in milligrammes the conviction was also upheld.

— in R. v. Souter a man owned a house and rented rooms where cannabis was smoked but as it couldn't be proved that he knew or turned a blind eye he was acquitted on appeal.

— in R. v. Moglord two girls aged 20 and 15 went to court for permitting smoking in their home. They lived with their parents who were away on holiday at the time. But the Judge ruled that they were not in 'legal possession' of the premises, so they got off.

— in R.v. Ashton-Rickhardt the police found a reefer in the defendant's car. Mr Ashton-Rickhardt said it had been left in his car by an acquaintance without his knowledge, and his appeal was allowed.

Miscellany

LEGAL HUMOUR

If you've got so far, I think you deserve a bit of legal humour. It isn't really a contradiction in terms, although funny stories about the law are indeed thin on the ground. Very often the biggest joke for a client is his bill, even if it wipes the grin off his face pretty quickly. I may as well tell them all. Here goes.

1. A prisoner was up for sentence before a crusty Judge. The Judge said 'Prisoner at the bar, before I pass sentence on you have you anything to say?' The prisoner, knowing that he was going down for a stretch anyway said under his breath 'No, f--- all'.

Judge 'What did he say?'

Barrister (very slowly and deliberately) 'He said "f--- all" m'lud.'

Judge 'That's funny, I could have sworn he said something.'

2. A solicitor was acting for a client who was borrowing money at an extortionate rate. In accordance with the usual routine, the solicitor for the lender sent the draft loan agreement to the borrower's solicitor, who saw that, due to a typing error, the clause providing for the usurious rate of interest, instead of reading 'and interest shall be paid at the rate of 40 per cent per *annum*' read 'and interest shall be paid at the rate of 40 per cent per *anum*'. When amendments are made to documents passing between solicitors they're normally made in red ink. The solicitor receiving the document chewed on his pen for a bit and then wrote in the margin of the document 'We were under the impression our client was paying through the nose'.

3. A Judge was hearing a rather odd case in which the defendant claimed to have had intercourse with a ghost. The Judge said incredulously 'I've never heard of anyone having intercourse with a ghost before'. At this a voice piped up from the back of the court: 'I have'. 'Then come up here and testify', said the Judge. The man went up to the witness box where the Judge repeated 'You say you have had intercourse with a ghost?' 'Oh no,' replied the man. 'I thought you said goat.'

4. A Judge who was a bit of a pompous know-all was hearing a drugs charge. A police witness produced a small phial of the heroin which was a vital piece of the evidence. 'Let me see it', said the Judge. The phial was given to him. 'Yes', he said, 'it looks like heroin.' He took out the small cork and held the phial close to his nose. 'Yes,' he went on, 'it smells like heroin.' He then held it to his lips and tasted it. 'Yes, and it tastes like heroin. Where was this exhibit found?' he asked the police officer. 'In', came the reply, 'the anus of the accused.'

5. An old lag had just had a sentence of seven years passed on him. 'My Lord', he wailed, 'I'm 74 and I'll never finish it.' 'Never mind', said the Judge in a kindly tone, 'try and do as much of it as you can.'

6. A solicitor and a doctor were chatting together at a party. The doctor was complaining about people who came up to him and asked for what amounted to a free medical consultation. 'I'm sure that you must get the same problems with people who want legal advice for free.' 'Absolutely right', replied the solicitor. 'What do you do about it?' asked the doctor. 'Well, I always listen carefully, give them my considered advice, and then I send them a bill the next day.' 'What a good idea', exclaimed the doctor. The next day he got a bill from the solicitor.

7. As a prisoner was leaving the dock after a stiff sentence, he shouted at the magistrate 'You bald old bastard!' The magistrate thought for a minute, then said as the prisoner was hustled out of court 'Well, at least he was right on two counts'.

8. A solicitor cabled his client after winning his case 'JUSTICE HAS BEEN DONE'. The client cabled back 'APPEAL AT ONCE'.